*Virtually Islamic*

**Religion, Culture and Society**

*Series Editors:*
Oliver Davies and Gavin Flood,
Department of Theology and Religious Studies,
University of Wales, Lampeter

**Religion, Culture and Society** is a series presented by leading scholars on a wide range of contemporary religious issues. The emphasis throughout is generally multicultural, and the approach is often interdisciplinary. The clarity and accessibility of the series, as well as its authoritative scholarship, will recommend it to students and a non-specialist readership alike.

# *Virtually Islamic*

## *Computer-mediated Communication and Cyber Islamic Environments*

GARY R. BUNT

UNIVERSITY OF WALES PRESS
CARDIFF
2000

British Library Cataloguing-in-Publication Data
A catalogue record for this book is available from the British Library.

ISBN 0-7083-1611-5 (paperback)
ISBN 0-7083-1612-3 (hardback)



Cover design by Olwen Fowler
Typeset at the University of Wales Press
Printed in Great Britain by Dinefwr Press, Llandybïe

‘For Yvonne, Kane and Tony’

# *Contents*

# *Acknowledgements*


The completion of this book would not have been possible, without the support of many individuals and institutions.

Encouragement in this book's development from colleagues at the Department of Theology, Religious Studies and Islamic Studies, University of Wales has been most welcome. The reader's comments and suggestions were also appreciated. This book is an extension of my doctoral work on decision-making processes in Islamic environments, and I am therefore (still) grateful to all those individuals and institutions who supported me on that project. These included the British Academy and the Spalding Trust.

I first introduced the 'Virtually Islamic' title for a plenary presentation at the 1998 British Society for Middle Eastern Studies (BRISMES) Annual Conference at Selly Oak College, Birmingham. The title appeared again when I provided a paper for the 1998 British Association for the Study of Religions (BASR) Annual Conference, held at Lampeter. The assistance of the conference organizers, who permitted me to introduce early versions of this research, is acknowledged.

Finally, the assistance of my family helped in the completion of this book: in particular, my parents provided their invaluable dimensions of support; Tony supplied useful angles in *Star Wars*' Cyberspace; and my wife Yvonne, who now converses in HTML, gave inspiration and encouragement. Kane Richard arrived and provided his unique form of support during the writing of this book.

Despite the valuable input of the above, the contents and any shortcomings of this book remain wholly the writer's responsibility.

Gary R. Bunt
Lampeter

# *Notes on the system of transliteration*

*Qur'ān*-ic/Islamic Arabic words can have several shades of meaning and interpretation. Similarly, many Islamic-Arabic words have different levels of meaning within different historical, intellectual, social, and/or colloquial contexts for Arabic speakers. The meaning of these words in other languages and contexts has led, in some cases, to further, varied understandings of a word or term, as can be seen on the Internet.

There are several different systems of transliteration available: for the purposes of this book, in order to provide an accessible method of transliteration, the model contained in Ian Richard Netton's book *A Popular Dictionary of Islam* (London: Curzon Press, 1991) has generally been adopted. Exceptions to this system have utilized and adapted the transliteration system contained within the *Encyclopedia of Islam: New Edition* system of transliteration of Arabic characters (*Encyclopedia of Islam: New Edition*, I (Leiden: E. J. Brill, 1960), p. xiii).

In the text of this book, the following exceptions to this system may apply:

(1) Anglicized Islamic-Arabic terminology i.e. 'mosque' for *masjid*.
(2) Proper names or terms of Islamic-Arabic origin following locally used or personal spellings or transliterations, where appropriate, i.e. 'Mohamed' for Muḥammad.
(3) Quotations from textual sources, which maintain their original transliterations.

## *Note on Internet references*

Website titles are in lower-case type in the Bibliography, together with Uniform Resource Locators (URLs). Unless otherwise stated, all Internet references were correct and links were functioning at the time of going to press. Given the fluid nature of the Internet, there is a likelihood of certain web pages 'relocating' or 'disappearing'. To counter this, references for this book will be continually updated on the Virtually Islamic webpage, which contains hyperlinks to all Internet sites referred to in this book.

**Virtually Islamic**

*http://www.virtuallyislamic.com*

# 1
# *Introduction*

A 'virtual world' is one created by digital illusion to provide a spatial sense of time and place containing phenomena that may or may not have a connection with 'reality'. In a virtual world, I can take off from a major airport in the aircraft of my choice, happily at the controls despite having no aeronautical training. I am safe in the knowledge that when my Boeing 747 enters a spin (which it inevitably does) the aircraft's fragmentation is virtual: I have been playing *Microsoft Flight Simulator*.[1]

To an extent, the Cyber Islamic Environments I visit are simulations too, representations of the real and also representations of the ideal. Some contain depictions of physical objects: mosques, sacred texts and images of Muslims. They also contain hard information and data, pure text without tangible mass. The Qur'ān in cyberspace does not physically resemble the Qur'ān on my desk. The difference between Cyber Islamic Environments and *Flight Simulator* is that the 'fragmentation' can impact on the real lives of individuals, at significant and at mundane levels.

The title *Virtually Islamic could* refer to an abstract world in which the illusory virtual contents are simply bits of data. Are the creators of this transcendent electronic space casting Islam in an idealized light? To what extent do Cyber Islamic Environments contain an edge of reality, which impact upon and represent actual people and issues? This book seeks to explore this issue.

*Virtually Islamic* can also refer to notions of identity. Is it possible to be 'digital' and 'Islamic', or is this, as some commentators would believe, an inherent contradiction? The intention of this book is to assess the impact of the many Islam-related sites on the Internet, and to explore how material on these sites represents and (potentially) influences Muslim and non-Muslim perspectives on Islam and Islamic issues. The Internet is a global provider of information, becoming more accessible to an increasing number of users. The process by which Islam-related material is filtered and presented has become a significant area of concern for many, including: those promoting specific understandings of Islam; those seeking to target and inform a young, educated audience; and academics and others seeking to monitor contemporary Islamic developments. The Internet can provide users with documentation, news, analysis and images that are conveyed rapidly, avoiding previously conventional channels.

Internet surfers have potential global access to millions of pages of information, of varying degrees of quality and utility, which can be located through the application of user-friendly technology. Given the appropriate equipment and pathways, information on any subject can, in theory, take only seconds to find. The Internet landscape, or 'cyberspace', contains a wide range of sites and perspectives on tens of thousands of subjects.[2] Many of these sites can be located through the use of search-engines and directories, which seek out specific information based on the input of parameters keyed in by the Internet user.[3] Football teams, cyber-shopping 'malls' and the stars of television 'soaps' coexist alongside governments, scientists and academics: the obscure nestles alongside the multinational, and diverse interests, platforms and belief-systems can be found. High-profile Internet profiles include: Buckingham Palace, the White House, the Vatican and 10 Downing Street. These all provide 'electronic tours', speeches and information, with the intention of receiving the appropriate public relations benefits in return!

The Internet is not just the domain of high-profile platforms. Any individual who has access to the appropriate computer hardware, software and telephone connection can create a personal Internet page (or webpage), the content of which may range from profound insights on the meaning of life through to a listing of favourite pets. The extent to which these enter the domain of vanity publishing, or indeed represent individuals who are 'shouting, but not being heard', is perhaps open to question. Even when a website is visited, its contents are not necessarily read throughout, and a surfer may only peruse the contents for a few seconds. To a website's owner, this still counts as a visit, which can be logged, monitored and tracked through the application of specific software. It might also be added to a total of hits or visits to a website, and applied as part of the site's publicity.

The nature of the Internet and its inherent accessibility means that webpages generally cannot be regulated (whether that is desirable or not). In some quarters, this has led to controversy regarding the contents of certain sites, for example neo-Nazi propaganda and pornography, and the attendant questions raised about freedom of information within this 'electronic democracy'. The thousands of Internet sites on offer in cyberspace are theoretically accessible, with few restrictions, to an international audience of hundreds of millions.

Opportunities to acquire knowledge about Islam and Muslims have emerged through utilization of this computer technology, including Internet sites, newsgroups, discussion groups and related services. From scholars to casual browsers, millions of people, Muslims and non-Muslims, now use the Internet as a primary source of information, so their approaches to Islam and Muslims may be influenced by what they locate on the Internet. Given the random nature of search-engines (discussed in this book), the procedure of searching for information about Islam in cyberspace can have conflicting results. The writer's wife, for example, was undertaking a research project and keyed in the words 'Muslim Women' on a search-engine. The result was links to thousands of pornographic sites, which may or may not have contained women who were Muslim but, given the descriptions on the search-engine listing, were certainly not undertaking 'Islamic acts'. This particular avenue of research was not pursued, although a single appropriate Muslim site was located low down on the listing.

Many use the Internet to convey their own interpretation of Islam and Islam-related issues. This has serious implications, given the diverse material and perspectives available, and the random way in which this information can be accessed. An individual's first experience of Islam in cyberspace is as likely to be a so-called 'schismatic group' or a 'radical' organization, as a mainstream 'orthodox' interpretation. It is not intended to imply any value-judgement through this statement, simply to suggest that when many Internet sites are not labelled in terms of their Islamic perspective, they may confuse readers and casual browsers.

In terms of understanding Islam, whether from an Islamic Studies/Religious Studies perspective *or not*, it is important to analyse developments on the Internet, as they are significant gauges of individual Muslim self-perception and specific group expression. Ahmed and Donnan's comments relating to Islamic Studies are particularly relevant when discussing Islam in cyberspace:

> . . . it is a critical moment in Islamic studies. We are at a cusp. It is time to point out the different features on the landscape – to point out where we were in the past and where we are heading for in the future.[4]

This present book emerged as a tangent from research, completed in 1995, discussing forms of decision-making issues in Islamic contexts.[5] Several fieldwork interviewees believed that the Internet (and related technology) would have the greatest impact of any single innovation or social change on Muslims during the next few decades. An interviewee at the International Islamic University in Islamabad suggested that:

> The development of this technology is going to make *ijtihād* [independent judgement based on Islamic sources] much easier for people. I don't have to look into this Encyclopaedia of Law or a book of comparative law or go to a concordance of Qur'ān and find out where in the world *ribā* [interest] is used – how many times. [For example] I simply need to move to my keyboard and tap in the keyboard, and it is going to give me how many places it appears within the Qur'ān, in *Hadīth*, in *Fiqh* books – and that is going to provide me with enormous material which can be analysed.
>
> Yet the poor human being's mind cannot be disregarded. With all this technological help, if I keep my mind locked and I never use it properly, no *ijtihād*. But I think modern gadgets make *ijtihād* much easier and with Internet it is going to be easier for me to verify my findings with a scholar in my micro-micro area who lives in Tunis. I just use my e-mail and reach him and verify from him and compare with him his observations and modify my views.[6]

Such comments led the writer to pay more attention to Islam in cyberspace. During this period, many significant technical developments have occurred, in particular the general shift from DOS text-only sites through to multimedia sites, and the improvement in browsers.[7] The writer acquired knowledge of the basic mechanics of the Internet through learning hypertext mark-up language (HTML) in order to construct Internet pages. Awareness of Internet issues came through browsing what has become a proliferation of Islam-related sites, and attempting to monitor and record significant developments.[8]

As a result of this interest, issues discussed in this book include:

- The nature of Islamic authority and guidance on the Internet.
- Applications of the Internet in fulfilling Islamic obligations.
- Islam and politics on the Internet.
- The future of the Internet in Islamic contexts.

The term 'computer-mediated communication' (CMC) is applied within the parameters of this discussion, and a number of studies have been made of the broad impact of so-called cyber-societies and the foundations of CMC.[9] Within this computer-mediated environment, key issues are raised regarding approaches to knowledge. The term 'environment' is itself of importance, given the perspective of the Canadian media theorist Marshall McLuhan, who discussed how different media forms influence and change behaviour:

> [So] the medium is the message is not a simple remark, and I've always hesitated to explain it. It really means a hidden environment of services created by an innovation. And the hidden environment of services is the thing that changes people. It is the environment that changes people, not the technology.[10]

McLuhan focuses on the impact of the medium, and its impact on human behaviour. Whilst he was talking in a pre-mass Internet/personal computer period, there is no doubt that his comments are relevant in terms of how patterns of thought have been changed for specific groups in the Muslim world. Methods of communication and dialogue have radically altered. The computer and modem have become a (or *the*) medium for analysing and discussing a wide range of Islam-related topics, transcending traditional barriers to communication.

In the context of this book, the forms of what could be described as Cyber Islamic Environments created by this technology are discussed in depth, to determine how they have integrated conventional paradigms of Muslim understanding with new patterns of behaviour. The sense of binding disparate individuals together seems significant when discussing various Internet activities. This may reflect Carey's comment: '. . . [But] the important element in cyberspatial social relations is the sharing of information. It is not sharing in the sense of the *transmission* of information that binds communities in cyberspace. It is the *ritual* sharing of information.'[11]

This 'ritual sharing' extends to the subject of ritual itself. Particular questions associated with Cyber Islamic Environments emerge, for example, relating to concepts of 'sacred space', the nature of Divine Revelation, and the nature of authority. Questions also arise linked with broad themes relating to research and debate in other cyber-linked fields of study, for example, on issues of identity, privacy, access and democracy in computer-mediated communication.[12]

Questions are raised as to how *computer media* are understood in these different frameworks and contexts. Strate, Jacobson and Gibson (echoing McLuhan) suggest that computer media: '. . . are best understood not just as means or agencies *through* which communication takes place, but as environments or scenes in which communication occurs'.[13] Undertaking research on (or within) such an electronic environment raises specific methodological considerations and a need to define specific parameters of study. Matters relating to technical issues, including the different configurations and types of hardware and software applied in the creation of sites, whilst perhaps interesting to some readers, are not covered in this book. The definitive book on which Muslim organizations and individuals use *Netscape Composer* or *Microsoft Front Page* as a basis for their webpages has yet to be written![14]

As well as surveying the 'information superhighway' and discussing related issues with scholars, material for this book has been acquired through e-mail interviews with those parties willing to engage in dialogue. Not every prospective interviewee was willing to participate, for a variety of reasons. These included: fears regarding their security; reluctance to engage in dialogue with a 'western'/non-Muslim 'academic'; and willingness only to engage in matters relating to the writer's soul and spiritual well-being, in this world and the world-to-come. However, several interviewees from diverse Muslim backgrounds were happy to contribute to this project, and provide valuable perspectives on issues relating to Islam and cyberspace. All these reactions inform this book. It is not the purpose of this book to make specific judgements as to the *validity* of information offered on the Internet, merely to delineate the Islamic Internet landscape. Whilst reference is made to e-mail, chat-rooms and other forms of electronic communication, the central focus of this book is the Internet.

The spectrum of Islamic understandings and content available online within Cyber Islamic Environments ranges from: propagation-orientated *Sunnī* (orthodox) and government-linked Islamic sites; through to a spectrum of *Ṣūfī* (Muslim mystics) and *Shī'a*-related sites; and non-orthodox, so-called 'schismatic' or 'Islamic sect' sites. Common threads of Muslim beliefs, and different shades of meaning, are represented in many of these sites. It is important to stress that these groups cannot be perceived as a monolithic entity, and that generalizations cannot be made relating to a single Cyber Islamic Environment, or any shared agendas. The issue of this diversity does not have to be construed negatively, neither is it an 'orientalist' construction intended to criticize Islam or Muslims. Separation is made in this book between Islam as defined in the Qur'ān and manifestations of what are Muslim or Islamic within contemporary contexts.

The term 'Islamic' in this book refers to any influence, for example, cultural, social, textual, political, Divine, in which the primary sources of Islam's formation or interpretation have contributed to an identity label. 'Islamic beliefs' are what an individual who describes him- or herself as Muslim undertakes in the name of Islam, whether that practice is approved by 'authorities' or not. The term 'Islamic environment' does not refer to a specific delineated geographical, historical or social entity: it is used here in the sense of a place where Islamic beliefs form an identity reference point (however marginal, secular or religious). For example, an Islamic environment could be a mosque, a house or street with Muslim residents, or an individual's sense of place and practice. The rigid criteria defining who is a Muslim utilized by various sources and schools of thought do not apply within this book.

When discussing Islam, care has to be taken to consider that there are many different interpretations of the concept of Islam.[15] In this book, awareness of the variables and diversity within Islam is useful, if there is equal consideration of those concepts that represent to many Muslims the universal factors in Islam. For example, the *Shahāda* or 'proclamation': 'There is no god but God, and Muḥammad is the Messenger of God.' This can be interpreted in different ways, but it is a universal factor in Islam. Similarly, Muslim scholars see the Qur'ān as constant and immutable, although it too may be interpreted in different ways, reflecting diverse influences and a multiplicity of systems and frameworks of understanding.

There can be considerable disparity between an individual's levels of understanding, belief and practice of Islam, and comprehension on, for example, a community, state and/or political level. Individuals and groups within communities in different Islamic environments present many opinions and approaches, and bring varied personal experiences toward what they define as 'Islam', 'Islamic' and 'Muslim'. Differing identities may be as much defined by cultural and traditional practices or external influences as by approaches to Islam. It is also recognized that there are shared beliefs, platforms and interests, for individuals and for those operating on specific agendas, which their advocates define as Islam, Islamic and/or Muslim. Some of these platforms go beyond small communities, to form national and/or international networks, or operate under the aegis of educational and social welfare programmes. Many of these are represented in Cyber Islamic Environments.

Many religious and socio-political platforms or individuals have chosen computer-mediated communication as a means of expressing diverse interpretations and understandings relating to Islam. Selective comparisons can be made between and within different Muslim interpretations represented on the Internet. Certain perspectives are *not* currently 'wired' into the Internet, for a variety of religious, economic, logistic, ideological and/or political reasons. The issue of representation is a critical one, for participants and observers. One webmaster in the United Arab Emirates noted that specific issues relating to representation of Islam appear on the Internet:

> There are serious risks too involved in propagation through the Web. There is no censorship of this 'open to all' medium. During the course of my surfing of Islamic sites, I have discovered that certain anti-Islamic elements, in the name of Islam, are trying to portray Islam negatively. They have even created web pages which in look and appearance are like Islamic pages but the information is mischievously provided to confuse and misguide the surfer.[16]

Questions concerning objectivity and bias in Islam-related Internet sources emerge. The freedom of information opportunities provided through the Internet mean that the browser is confronted by diverse and often conflicting opinions relating to Islam and Muslims, a microcosm of the non-digital world. The case of a non-Muslim platform establishing a site based around fabricated verses from the Qur'ān caused controversy in 1998, and is documented in this book.

Computer-mediated environments provide a means for diverse Muslim platforms to express their opinions on a variety of matters, from sacred to profane. As will be seen in this book, many of these viewpoints would be marginalized in other media. Computer-mediated environments provide a platform for their views, which can take the form of sermons and articles as well as interpretations of the news. In a discussion on the impact of the audio cassette on 'political Islam', Eickelman and Piscatori noted:

> The sermons of Lebanon's Shaykh Fadlallah, Egypt's Shaykh 'Abd al-Hamid Kishk, and Malaysia's Haj Hadi Awang are widely available beyond their country of origin and are often found in Europe and America where Muslim students are located. 'Voiced Islam' (*al-Islam al-sawti*) has thus become a formidable force rivalling 'print Islam'.[17]

The concept of voiced Islam has now extended, with the wide availability of *RealPlayers* (and similar software), that allow audio material to be downloaded and played on computers.[18] There are many examples of *al-Islam al-sawti*, in English and other languages which, whilst not having the same catchment areas as cheap audio cassettes, will inevitably have an impact amongst those with access to computers (and the inclination to browse and download such sermons).

As interest in computer-mediated computing increases, there is a need to monitor developments and shifts in attitude on various

Cyber Islamic Environments. Technical innovations, based on developments including video-streaming, *RealPlayers* and video interactivity, mean that many aspects of Cyber Islamic Environments will have radically altered by 2010. As well as requiring detailed and consistent research to maintain awareness of contemporary issues, researchers will need to maintain records (digital or otherwise) of these developments. This book forms a snapshot of cyberspace activity relating to Islam, charting formative aspects in Cyber Islamic Environments up to and including 1999. Whilst not a history of these sites, this book provides an analysis of their roles, their evolution and anticipated impacts. In terms of cyberspace in general, and Cyber Islamic Environments in particular, rapid developments can occur in a relatively compressed time period, with new sites emerging every week. Mitra made an important methodological consideration when discussing the Internet:

> At best it is possible to identify a period of time and obtain a snapshot of the image being produced and circulated. That conclusion is neither binding nor exhaustive since, ever-metamorphosing and ever-growing, the 'nature of the Internet beast' continues to change every minute (literally), undermining any claim of authenticity that researchers can have of their reading of the network discourse. Researchers need to be aware of this, and thus be cautious and prepared to accept the fact that the image is indeed transitional and is bound to change with time and the appearance of new community members.[19]

The Islamic Internet landscape changes frequently, with new sites emerging on a daily basis. Some very proactive players change their content and format regularly, attempting to draw readers to their message(s) in order to establish links or a sense of community. Howard Rheingold, who anticipated the aspects of interconnectivity and dialogue possible in a digital world, explored this concept of a 'virtual community' in its early stages. Whilst he was particularly drawn to 'alternative' post-hippy culture, many of his projections relating to interconnectivity have a resonance in Cyber Islamic Environments.[20]

Whereas Rheingold in his early writings was able to provide an overview of virtual communities, now it is very difficult, and the analysis of the Internet increasingly requires specialization of specific fields of interest, such as 'Islam on the Internet'. This is why it is important at this stage to discuss Cyber Islamic Environments, especially as they now are expanding so rapidly:

> Compared to only 3 years ago, the Islamic related web-scene seems to have exploded like mushrooms. As a Muslim, I view the other web sites as 'one' network complementing and supporting each other in their work. However, the reality of inter-co-operation among the sites still needs a lot of work and co-ordination. Nevertheless, the inter-connection among the sites are developing quite naturally [*sic*]. There are sites who are eagerly and genuinely trying to promote this family-directed goal. On the other hand, unfortunately, there are some sites portraying negative messages either intentionally or unconsciously, showing an unhealthy internecine 'web war' between different ideals or methods or even theological differences.[21]

Given this pattern of growth and interconnectivity, it is anticipated that specialization in Cyber Islamic Environments is now becoming necessary, and that the field is an important one for future academic research.

Many individuals and organizations at local and national levels throughout the world are becoming aware that the Internet is an increasingly relevant medium with which to communicate their perspectives on Islam and Muslim issues. For example, in Iran, Seyyed Ḥassan Khumaynī (Khomeini) stated at the June 1998 inauguration of an Internet site devoted to his grandfather Āyatullāh Rūḥūllāh Khumaynī:

> I am sure that with love, faith and commitment, the use of technology and modern science have opened a new window to the world so that people around the world would become more and more acquainted with the genuine culture of Islam and its capabilities . . .
>
> . . . through advancing our perceptions and strengthening our beliefs, we can be made capable of dispensing the responsibilities assigned to us effectively by Imam Khomeini and conquer new horizons in the lofty ideals of Islam and the Islamic Revolution.[22]

Whilst Rūḥūllāh Khumaynī made good use of the audio cassette, his grandson promotes this specific interpretation of Shī'a Islam through the Internet.

Questions also arise as to what extent, if at all, a 'digital *umma*' (the writer's term) is emerging or being promoted. The term *umma* can represent the concept of a single Muslim community, idealized in Islamic sources in the descriptions of the first Muslim community formed during the lifetime of the Prophet Muḥammad (570–632 CE/Common Era) and extended to describe a 'single Muslim people'. In Cyber Islamic Environments, reference is frequently made to '(cyber) identities' that integrate this *umma* concept. This raises a number of interesting theoretical questions, which this book seeks to introduce to the reader:

- Is this 'digital *umma*' a 'real' and/or 'imagined' phenomenon?
- Does cyberspace create an *idealized* sense of Muslim identity (or identities), compared with the reality? What impact can this have on individuals and communities, especially those situated in 'hostile' situations?
- How do Cyber Islamic Environments reflect traditions, 'orthodoxy', 'messages', individuality and pluralism in Islamic contexts?
- Do Cyber Islamic Environments on the Internet represent, in certain contexts, the loss of traditional centres of knowledge and power, manifestations of transnationalism where conventional borders, controls and authorities are electronically circumnavigated?[23]

The Internet is an environment where participation *can* be 'identity-less'.[24] In theory power can be decentralized, although in practice in several Islamic contexts, power and control of the web is strictly controlled. Questions arise as to whether this represents what Hamid Mowlana describes as 'the spirit of globalism, the satisfaction of achieved goals, participatory democracy, realization of time value, voluntary community, and a synergetic economy'.[25]

There are individuals and organizations seeking to project a 'definitive' concept on the Internet relating to Islam and its interpretation/implementation, frequently associated with a specific exegesis of Islamic primary source material. This material includes:

- God's Revelation to Muḥammad contained in the Qur'ān;
- the sayings and actions of Muḥammad (*aḥādīth* and *sunna*) contained in various collections and interpretations;

- legalistic interpretations of these primary sources, contained in diverse collections of jurisprudence projected through various schools;
- philosophical and esoteric perspectives on Islam;
- other diverse authorities, perhaps associated with regional, ethnic and/or cultural issues, interpretations and interpreters.

The domination of certain political-religious 'Islamic' viewpoints, seeking to represent themselves as *the* authentic voice of Islam on the Internet, is a phenomenon considered in this book. The selectivity and objectivity of certain sites, in terms of the material they prove and their links to other sites, is illuminating (in particular, the omissions, deliberate or otherwise). Whilst several, potentially conflicting, Internet sites project themselves as ultimate authorities on Islam, others do not directly suggest this authority, and may project instead authority focused on a specific sector within the Islamic spectrum, perhaps of a trans-global nature, crossing political and geographical boundaries. This phenomenon can be linked with discussions on so-called postmodernity and globalization: 'By "globalisation", scholars refer to the way in which, under contemporary conditions especially, relations of power and communication are stretched across the globe, involving compression of time and space and a recomposition of social relationships.'[26]

Traditional structures of authority and power can be reconfigured within the Cyber Islamic Environments, and new forces of authority are emerging. This book addresses the issue of the extent to which the Internet is '[G]lobalizing the local, [and] localizing the global' within Islamic contexts.[27] Whilst analysing and observing this pluralism and globalization in the Internet landscape, perhaps a digital phenomenology of Islam can be constructed, reflecting what Ninian Smart describes as the 'ideas and practices which have moved people'.[28] These could include cultural systems, conceptualization, theorization and practices of Islam and Muslims.[29]

Huma Aḥmad's article 'Muslims on the Internet' confronts the issues of Muslim representation on the Internet from the perspective of a webpage author:

> . . . Muslim chat rooms and MUDs such as ISNET are especially the hang-outs for high school and college age Muslims . . . it is also highly addictive and highly unregulated. Flirting and private online relationships are pervasive. Also, among some of the Internet chat channels such as Channel Islam is a very anti-Kuffar [anti-unbeliever] sentiment, with scripts such as 'Muslim pulls out a baseball bat, Muslim smashes Jew over the head, Muslim wipes off the blood.' The few who control the Islam channel kick and ban arbitrarily whoever disagrees with their opinion or definition of Islam. Where the potential for Dawah [propagation of Islam] is at its greatest, the reputation of being narrow-minded and hypocritical has increased clashes and hacking between even the different Muslim channels . . .
>
> No scholars or Sheikhs are present on any of these mediums. There are no authorities or any kind of collaborative effort on the part of Muslims. Advice and Fatwas to non-Muslims and Muslims are given out by basically anyone and dangerously lacking in references or scholarly wisdom and knowledge.
>
> Despite everything, there are many positives [*sic*] to Muslims being on the Internet. In fact it has influenced many in good ways, from just increasing their Iman [faith] and knowledge to eventually leading people to Shahadah [proclaim Islam]. This new technology has been a breakthrough in communication among Muslims.[30]

Examination of some of the phenomena associated with Islam and the Internet reveals some interesting manifestations of Muslim belief-systems, and an integration of digital technology with the primary foundations of Islam. For example, prayer, spirituality, the contemplative quest and ideas of the sacred are all available online. Questions emerge as to whether it is possible to have a religious experience through computer-mediated communication. Can Cyber Islamic Environments produce the sense of religious essence, the transcendent, the numinous, the Other, what Otto describes as *mysterium tremendum et fascinaus*?[31] Is there a digital theophany, if one approaches the term as relating to the Greek word *pathos*, providing a sense of religious experience and emotion: 'a religious emotion aroused by meditation about God'?[32] Certainly they could be a medium through which such experiences could be generated, perhaps through listening to sacred texts or through observing the experiences of others.

Such an experience *could* be attained through listening to the Qur'ān, which is well represented on the Internet, through high-quality recitations available for downloading. New concepts relating to accessing texts emerge in religious 'cyber environments'. The Qur'ān can be accessed (and copies manipulated) by anyone with a modem. Members of different religions (and those without allegiance) can explore and discuss sacred texts online. Dialogues can take place anonymously, exploring different forms of human religious experience: the experiential, the emotional, and forms of what Smart describes as 'inner dynamism'.[33]

Clearly, there are numerous social, political, technological and religious issues associated with Cyber Islamic Environments and computer-mediated communication. This writer's personal perspective emerges from a framework of multidisciplinary/interdisciplinary Islamic and Religious Studies, drawing upon several subject areas. It is intended that this book will provide an overview of the subject, which can be drawn upon by specialists and students of other disciplines, as well as general readers, whatever their personal belief framework.

Computer-mediated communication has long-term implications in shaping Muslim communities, in both minority and majority settings. New issues related to the Internet continue to emerge, as more of the Muslim world (or worlds) become 'wired'. Cyber Islamic Environments may influence specific sectors within Muslim societies, including an educated élite with access to computers. This may impact on other sectors of societies indirectly, depending on the influence and prestige of networks and individuals accessing computers. This is especially true if ideas or resources projected within Cyber Islamic Environments cause major or minor shifts in outlook relating to perceived Muslim identity or common issues which go beyond conventional borders: these projections may or may not be contained in other media.

The rapid shifts and changes that occur in Cyber Islamic Environments require recording and monitoring. This book is a modest attempt to initiate this process, and to establish an introductory dialogue on the subject. With new Internet sites emerging daily, and existing sites regularly changing, this book cannot provide a full picture of Islamic thought and belief in cyberspace. It is intended that this overview of Cyber Islamic Environments will offer some insight into contemporary manifestations of Islam within and outside computer-mediated environments, and provide a tool for the reader's own interpretation and understanding of Islamic material acquired online. As a subtext, the book also seeks to raise considerations relating to methodological approaches and information-gathering in cyberspace.

The nature and size of Cyber Islamic Environments require interdisciplinary approaches, and many potential pathways (or distractions) have emerged in the pursuit of this research. It is hoped that the reader will follow those cyber-alleyways that time and resources did not allow for this specific project, and perhaps alert the writer to the results of their exploration. In recognizing that this is radically new subject matter, this book provides an overview, rather than a scientifically controlled analysis of a 'controlled group' (or groups) of Internet sites. It is hoped that the readers, from whatever background, will contribute and enhance the dialogue, through the medium of the web, and via an especially created website for links and reactions to *Virtually Islamic: Computer-Mediated Communication and Cyber Islamic Environments*.[34]

# 2

# *Primary forms of Islamic expression online*

## 2.1 Introduction

If there is a 'digital *umma*' or Muslim community in cyberspace, then the Qur'ān, as the Revelation of God received by Muḥammad (c. 570–632 CE) via the Angel Gabriel, would be a central focus of any computer-mediated activity in the name of Islam. As a text, the Qur'ān has a significant presence in Cyber Islamic Environments, with thousands of links to diverse digital versions (and extracts), in a number of translations. The Qur'ān in cyberspace also represents a continuity of the obligation of *da'wa* or propagation of Islam.

Contemporary examples of *da'wa* include varied print media such as books, newspapers and pamphlets, together with audio-visual media such as radio and television broadcasts, and recorded cassettes (and increasingly videos) of sermons, Qur'ānic recitations and entertainment incorporating an Islamic message. The definition of *da'wa* can also incorporate aspects of personal and community behaviour, perhaps based around the example of the Prophet Muḥammad, thus creating a model that others might seek to emulate. At the micro-level, *da'wa* is still seen as part of a human interaction process, where individual Muslims and organizations seek to propagate Islam, often in association with a particular perspective or interpretation. The Internet now forms part of this process, with the Qur'ān a central feature of Islamic computer landscapes.

The intended audience may be non-Muslim, although *da'wa* can also have the sense of developing the beliefs of existing Muslims. Clearly, this has some implications in terms of the designs of Internet interfaces, as to whether an individual surfing a site is familiar with the Qur'ān or not. Many sites centred on the Qur'ān intend to establish a digital presence for this sacred text, in line with websites from other religions. They may appeal to the curious non-Muslim, existing Muslims, and/or Muslims from outside the specific traditional and interpretative practices endorsed by a website's authors.

## 2.2 Locating the Qur'ān online

Approaching the Qur'ān on the Internet can be a very different experience from approaching a paper copy. An online Qur'ān is 'searchable'; this means that key words can be isolated or listed, for example on a particular theme. Like a printed copy, it may be translated from Arabic, perhaps with a particular emphasis in the mind of the translator; however, it is interactive and multi-dimensional, given that it potentially can be heard in Arabic, whilst browsed in English with a simultaneous Arabic text version.

The status of a printed or written Qur'ān in the eyes of Muslims may be that of a sacred and sanctified physical object, to be approached and held in ritual cleanliness. In a sense, an online Qur'ān cannot be physically touched – although, in reality, pages can be downloaded, printed and integrated into other textual forms which may not be seen as appropriate by some. Whilst issues surrounding the educational benefits are clear within Islamic sources, the implications of electronic versions of the Qur'ān are still to be agreed by decision-makers. Given that many organizations, platforms and 'authorities' promote the dissemination of the Qur'ān on the Internet, this would appear to be an implicit endorsement of its electronic form.

Islam is focused on the power of the word. Reading and recitations provide a central mandate. The first word that Muḥammad received from God was *'Iqrā* or 'read':

> Proclaim! [or Read!] in the name of thy Lord and Cherisher, who created –
> Created man, out of a [mere] clot of congealed blood:
> Proclaim! And thy Lord is Most Bountiful, –
> He Who taught [the use of] the Pen, –
> Taught man that which he knew not.[1]

Both *'iqrā* and *qur'ān* are derivations from the verb *qara'a*, which means 'to read' or 'to recite'. The Qur'ān consists of the Divine Revelation Muḥammad received from God – via the Angel Jibrīl (Gabriel) – between the years 610 and 632 CE.

Muḥammad is perceived as the medium for the Revelation, rather than its author, and information contained in traditional sources relating to Muḥammad's life place a firm emphasis on the very human reactions he expressed upon receiving the first Revelation. Muḥammad was a resident of Mecca, a city whose fortune, prior to the arrival of Islam, was based on its strategic trading position, and its pantheistic pilgrimage site, the *Ka'ba*. The origins of the *Ka'ba* or 'holy house' are described in the Qur'ān as being associated with the prophet Ibrāhīm (Abraham), giving Islam a strong link with Judaism and Christianity, and providing Muḥammad with a legitimacy as a 'final' Prophet.

Muḥammad faced considerable opposition in many quarters, when he cautiously started to explain the Revelation he had received to others. Muḥammad faced situations of conflict and adversity, which were often tempered by the contextual Revelation he received, in order to answer questions and solve difficulties. The Revelation was always in what is defined as a pure form of Arabic, with its poetic metre and divinely inspired content. Many accusations were made during Muḥammad's lifetime that he was not a prophet, but a poet or a madman. Answers to these criticisms, and articles on Muḥammad's nature, are subjects with considerable currency in contemporary Cyber Islamic Environments.

The Qur'ān was recorded in a medium very different from the digital world: as it emerged, Muḥammad and his followers memorized the text, either through memory and/or through its recording in writing – for example, as fragmentary inscriptions on wood, bones and stones. Muḥammad was said to receive an annual visit from Gabriel, during which the Qur'ān would be repeated to him. According to 'orthodox' understanding, the definitive collection of these fragments was compiled after Muḥammad's death by the Prophet's scribe Zayd ibn Thābit (d. *c.* 655), as several versions were in circulation.[2] Minor textual differences were seen as possessing the potential to cause controversy, and damage efforts made to create a single Muslim community or *umma*.

The deaths in battle of over seventy Qur'ānic 'memorizers' heightened the need for a definitive, inviolable textual version of the Qur'ān, which could be accurately copied and distributed in the rapidly expanding Islamic context. This single volume (or *mushāf*) was intended to reproduce the Revelation without excluding any word, term or even diacritical point of Arabic. This would guarantee that a Qur'ān in Damascus would be identical in every way to a Qur'ān in Mecca. This would also mean that it was universally recited in the same way – at least in terms of content (although certain variations in recitation style did emerge, based on regional and cultural factors). These stylistic variations can be located online.

The consistency of the Qur'ān's Arabic text remains today. However, as can be seen on the Internet, there are variations in terms of meanings ascribed to the text (or portions of it). Cultural, historical, philosophical and political factors have influenced translations and interpretations. A translation of the meaning of the Qur'ān – such as the texts available online – might not possess the same status as an Arabic Qur'ān, although in many non-Arabic language contexts, a translation of the text's meaning is printed alongside the Arabic. Certain verses may be seen to require exegesis, in order to determine the real meaning, and the training of scholars has been encouraged in order to promote understanding. Controversy has arisen relating to the status of such scholars in various Muslim environments, and this has spilled over into cyberspace – when examining the pronouncements of various 'authorities' online.

The Qur'ān has a format that may appear complex to outsiders. Its content is not presented thematically, neither is it presented in relation to a chronological pattern or context. The order of chapters (or *Suwar*) within the Qur'ān is based upon length.[3] After a short opening *sūra*, the Qur'ān has 113 other *suwar* ranging from the longest to the shortest. Scholars have determined that even within one chapter a *sūra* may contain Revelation that appeared in different contexts and phases (during the 610–32 period). It was not intended simply to be a 'book' read from cover to cover: rather, it could be browsed and information gleaned from it, often in response to specific questions of interpretation. It was also a text that was memorized, and could similarly be drawn upon by a *ḥāfiz* – one who had learnt the Qur'ān by heart. In many ways, this 'browsability' resembles a computer hypertext, searchable for themes and subjects through an interface: whereas that might traditionally be an *imām* or a scholar (*'ālim*), in contemporary contexts, the interface can also be digital.[4]

Contextual evaluation has significance, due to its subsequent application in Islamic legal frameworks based on *sharī'a* (or law based on Islamic sources). Interpretation of the context of specific *suwar* is often associated with a separate, complementary (and hierarchically lower) source to the Qur'ān – the sayings (*aḥādīth*) and actions (*sunna*) of Muḥammad. These were collected in diverse volumes by networks of scholars, and classified according to the credibility of their transmitters and the 'authenticity' of the material. Frequently, they are sourced in a comparative format alongside very similar sayings, perhaps with slight differences in emphases and/or different chains of transmission. These sources and factors associated with them are particularly relevant to those seeking to emulate Muḥammad's behaviour, or to create a society based upon an interpretation of the Qur'ān.

Given that the Qur'ān contains 6,235 *āyāt* or verses (singular: *āya*) with different emphases and contextual applications (devotional, legalistic, esoteric, instructional), the science of discerning the complete meaning, as far as humanly possible, of the Revelation received by Muḥammad required access to a broad range of sources. Specialization within legal and decision-making frameworks emerged – in part due to the complexity and size of the Islamic primary source corpus, built around the Qur'ān and its interpretations. Historical and ideological influences also led to diverse understandings of what it meant to be Muslim and how Islam was defined, albeit with consistent factors and features threading through these definitions. Many of these aspects of diversity are reflected when examining Cyber Islamic Environments. Focusing on English-language sources, questions emerge as to which translations of the meaning of the Qur'ān appear on various listings, and what are their particular emphases? Can the Revelation be presented in translation on its own, without a commentary? If so, what impact does this have upon the casual 'surfer' or browser of the Internet?

Questions also emerge of *why* it is seen as important to have Muslim primary sources online. How has the influence of other religions impacted upon the motivation of web-authors (authors perhaps operating separately, or as part of a group)? Muslims and non-Muslims identified the potential applications of electronic Qur'āns, which could be searched for key words and phrases. File Transfer Protocols (FTP) meant that, even in the early days of computer-mediated communication, an electronic Qur'ān text (in translation) could be downloaded onto a computer. Such downloads appeared, provided by Muslim platforms and individuals, and/or by academic institutions. These would list the Qur'ān in listings that might also contain other religious textual sources (this was true of Muslim and non-Muslim listings).[5] Such sources were 'free' in the sense that they could be accessed by those with the appropriate equipment, although connection times and download speeds meant that accessing a site and downloading the material was potentially expensive. Sites could also be 'searched' for particular material. Similar options emerged within the *aḥādīth* corpus.

An early example was that of the Humanities Text Initiative of the University of Michigan. This describes itself as: 'an umbrella organization for the acquisition, creation, and maintenance of electronic texts'.[6] Its foundation in 1994 was the successor to an earlier project, instigated in 1990. Religious texts listed include several versions of the Bible, the Book of Mormon, and the Qur'ān translation produced by M. H. Shakir.[7] The online version incorporates a number of different search formats:

- 'simple searches', through which a single word or phrase can be located in the entire text;
- 'proximity searches' allow for the location of two or three words or phrases;
- 'Boolean searches' seek combinations of two or three words in a specific section of the Qur'ān;
- a browser allows for individual chapters to be selected and perused.

Whilst this was not an acknowledged Muslim site, it drew from and reproduced a widely recognized translation of the Qur'ān.

Recognition of the problems associated with providing Qur'ān translations online is indicated on a long-established site produced by the Muslim Students Association of the University of Southern California (MSA of USC). This includes diverse resources, such as texts, images and audio files. It provides three translations of the Qur'ān: Shakir's, 'Abdullāh Yūsuf 'Alī's, and Marmaduke Moḥammad Pickthall's. These are popular translations, widely available in printed form, although the MSA issues the following warning:

> Please keep in mind that ANY translation of the Qur'ān will most definitely contain errors (e.g. see our online list of corrections). We have provided three translations here to emphasize this point. In its natural language (Arabic), the Qur'ān is the direct Word of Allah (God) to mankind through the prophet Muhammad (peace be upon him). Any translation of the Qur'ān no longer retains that 'official' and perfect status, however it can be tremendously helpful to beginning students wanting to learn more about Islam.
>
> We would strongly encourage those [who] want to learn about Islam to purchase a hardcopy of the Qur'an but with the following conditions:
>
> - get one with commentary (tafseer)
> - make sure the tafseer is scholarly (e.g. references to reasons behind a verse, references to hadith and sunnah, etc.).[8]

Assumptions cannot be made that Arabic-speakers will necessarily discern the appropriate interpretation of the Qur'ān either, given that Qur'ān-ic Arabic differs from Modern Standard Arabic, and that there are numerous dialectical forms of the language. There is considerable discussion (including online) as to which commentary or *tafsīr* is appropriate.

The MSA of USC applied Muslim networking resources in copying the translations from the Islamic Computing Centre, a London-based commercial company. The MSA also recommends that a *tafsīr,* written by the 'reform'-orientated writer Sayyid Abul A'lā Mawdūdī (1903–79), is consulted by those utilizing the online Qur'ān. The promotion of Mawdūdī is itself interesting, given that he founded the Jamā'at-i Islāmī movement in the Indian subcontinent in the early 1940s. The movement promotes a specific Qur'ān- and Sunnī-centric interpretation of Islam as a 'way of life', influenced by Wahhābī doctrine and Saudi Arabian theologians, and has some political and institutional influence in Pakistan. Mawdūdī wrote extensive commentaries on the Qur'ān, synthesizing his interpretation with political concerns. It is reproduced widely both within Cyber Islamic Environments and in print, and translated into several languages (including

English). *Jamā'at-i Islāmī*, discussed later in this book, has networking influence in certain 'reform'-centred movements and organizations, for example, in Malaysia and the United Kingdom. The application of terms such as 'reform' and 'modernity' themselves have diverse implications and interpretations.

An alternative reform-centred influence in Qur'ān translations is located in a Qur'ān translation by Muḥammad Taqī-ud-Dīn Al-Hilālī and Muḥammad Muḥsin Khān of the Islamic University, Al Madīna Al-Munawwara, Saudi Arabia.[9] This provides, as part of the text, comments and translations relating to specific meanings based upon other scholars and historians, for example, the *aḥādīth* collection of Muḥammad b. Ismā'īl al-Bukhārī (810–70). Whilst this may be described as 'clarification', there is an implicit subtext within the translation, essentially in its focus on a stylization of 'monotheism', and often in its antipathy to forms of esoteric interpretation. The translation of *Sūrat Al-Naḥl* provides one example:

> Verily, Allâh enjoins Al-Adl (i.e. justice and worshipping none but Allâh Alone – Islâmic Monotheism) and Al-Ihsân (i.e. to be patient in performing your duties to Allâh, totally for Allâh's sake and in accordance with the Sunnah (legal ways) of the Prophet SAW in a perfect manner), and giving (help) to kith and kin (i.e. all that Allâh has ordered you to give them e.g., wealth, visiting, looking after them, or any other kind of help, etc.): and forbids Al-Fahshâ' (i.e all evil deeds, e.g. illegal sexual acts, disobedience of parents, polytheism, to tell lies, to give false witness, to kill a life without right, etc.), and Al-Munkar (i.e all that is prohibited by Islâmic law: polytheism of every kind, disbelief and every kind of evil deeds, etc.), and Al-Baghy (i.e. all kinds of oppression), He admonishes you, that you may take heed.[10]

The emphasis on examples *within the text* presents a specific interpretation of the Qur'ān, holistically as part of the corpus – a factor that may be confusing to the casual browser. Compare the above translation with that of Shakir: 'Surely Allah enjoins the doing of justice and the doing of good (to others) and the giving to the kindred, and He forbids indecency and evil and rebellion; He admonishes you that you may be mindful.'[11]

Issues relating to linguistic style also emerge, for example in the application of the Pickthall translation of the same *āya*: 'Lo! Allah enjoineth justice and kindness, and giving to kinsfolk, and forbiddeth lewdness and abomination and wickedness. He exhorteth you in order that ye may take heed.'[12] It is not the purpose here to determine which translation is superior, but clearly format and comprehension issues arise. All are online, and have variations in meaning. The issue similarly emerges in other online translations in other languages, and is clearly part of the wider issue surrounding translation of sources.[13]

The Pickthall source cited above appears on an electronic search facility developed by Richard L. Goerwitz of Brown University Scholarly Technology Group in the United States. This allows for more sophisticated search and analysis, including comparative versions of Yūsuf 'Alī, Shakir and Pickthall. Searches can be undertaken on the basis on specific words or *suwar* titles.[14] Other versions available online include searches based on subject matter.[15]

The Qur'ān can also be accessed in the form of audio files, allowing a recitation to be downloaded and played (*sūra* by *sūra*) if the surfer has access to appropriate computer hardware and software. Whereas the Qur'ān search-engines provide hard copy that is also available in conventional printed forms, the audio versions of the Qur'ān allow the individual browser to access material that may have been especially recorded for the web. There is a precedent of Qur'ān recitation recordings being made available in other formats, such as audio cassette, video and CDs; this in itself was seen in the past as an innovation, and cited as dangerous. During the 1960s, the broadcasting of the Qur'ān on television was strongly opposed by some quarters in Saudi Arabia.[16] Now any surfer, Muslim or non-Muslim, can download a choice of recitation. Many reputable *mutajwīd* or reciters are now available online, alongside recordings of calls to prayer and other Islamic recordings. Versions of the *adhān* recorded by *Mu'adhdhin* (muezzin) in Mecca and Medina can have a particular resonance and emotional appeal, especially for Muslim browsers.

Many examples are located on the Radio Al-Islam site.[17] This is a dedicated audio project, offering a broad range of recitations. Radio Al-Islam is linked to the IslamiCity website, an extremely comprehensive and detailed selection of original material produced by the Islamic Information Network, which presents a

Sunnī-centric perspective. According to its register of visitors, IslamiCity had received 1,115,487 visits from browsers in the period from 24 October 1997 to 26 October 1998 – and more than 24 million hits (or 'clicks' on links). The technical indices of the site suggest that a considerable percentage of these hits were for the Qur'ān-related links.[18] IslamiCity possesses one of the most important URLs (Uniform Resource Locators or 'web addresses') relating to Cyber Islamic Environments (*http://www.islam.org*), and is a central point of reference for any surfer accessing Islam-related material. Paradoxically, IslamiCity's disadvantages include the sheer bulk of material contained on the site. This can present difficulties in terms of ease of navigation; the site's excessive use of frames and images requires a substantial, and potentially expensive, download period for the user (and a lack of accessibility for users of less sophisticated machines).

Radio Al-Islam claimed to have provided the entire Qur'ān on the Internet in audio format for the first time on 14 April 1997. The recitation is credited as a recording of Shaikh Khalil Hussary.[19] The interface lists the individual *sūra* numbers and titles (in English and in Roman transliteration), and during 1998 offered English audio files of selected *suwar.* In order to test the system, the writer downloaded *Sūrat al-Nas,* one of the short *suwar* (discussed above). The audio channel produced a high audio-quality recitation, taking a few minutes to download.[20]

One ethical issue for consideration was when the recording stopped, and there was a long and inappropriate silence during the *sūra*. Many Muslims would deem a 'broken' prayer as being faulty, and there are several references to different definitions of incomplete prayer contained in Islamic sources. If a Muslim was praying alongside the recording, as part of religious obligation, the purity of intention to pray might suggest that such a technically induced silence would not 'damage' the prayer, but necessitate a repeated portion of prayer. Questions may emerge as to the validity and application of *suwar* recordings in Cyber Islamic Environments.

Upon clicking Radio Al-Islam's link for the audio file, the interface provided a page dedicated to the *sūra* – including the text in Arabic, scanned into the page as an image, rather than provided in an Arabic HTML (hypertext mark-up language) format for easier browsing. The page also provided a hyperlink to

Yūsuf 'Alī's English translation, and to Mawdūḍī's commentary on a *sūra* (from the MSA site discussed above).[21] These allow for simultaneous perusal of texts, depending on the level of knowledge of the surfer.

Several other options are available within Cyber Islamic Environments in order to locate recitations, and similar issues apply. Providers of these services require extensive web space in order to facilitate these recordings online. One pioneering version of the Qur'ān in audio format appeared under the Cyber Muslim banner, an ambitious project providing textual and audio versions of the Qur'ān. This system included a 'HyperQur'aan' with searchable indices in different languages, together with related audio files. The author, Mas'ood Cajee, promoted Islam through various 'tours', 'hosted' by Selim the CyberMuslim. This specific site, although influential on subsequent Cyber Islamic Environments, was no longer available at the time of writing.

Cyber Islamic Environments have evolved and improved over time, and CyberMuslim was in a way superseded by Radio Al-Islam and other websites. Cyber Muslim was an individual's project, similar to that of 'Hamo's Homepage' – an extensive selection of Islam-related material, including Qur'ān recitations, juxtaposed with medical data reflecting the author's personal interests. As technology stood in 1999, it seemed a lengthy process to download the high-quality recitation provided by Shaykh Abdulrahman As-Suday. Whilst not negating Hamo's Homepage as a resource, stylistic aspects of this specific recitation, such as the Shaykh's rapid pronunciation, make it less accessible for newcomers, and there is no text (in English or Arabic) to follow. This provides some indication relating to the perceived potential audience, perhaps suggesting those with existing familiarity with the Qur'ān, rather than those new to the text.

Cyber Islamic Environments expose Muslims to 'new' recitations, providing options for those with access to the Internet to hear Qur'ānic recitations in work, home and college environments; the cost of downloading such material may mean that this is a supplement to other commercially available recordings, available in other formats. As a basis for future services, when download times are substantially reduced and sound quality further improved, these sites demonstrate that

Muslim interests will already possess a substantial and technically proficient presence online, in terms of primary resources.

There are many other links to audio material within Cyber Islamic Environments (some of which will be discussed later in this book). The stylistic variations in recitation could be compared and contrasted by surfers with sufficient expertise. Technically, too, the recordings vary in audio quality. However, recordings that have obviously not been made to professional audio standards have intrinsic merit of their own, including the sense that the surfer is obtaining something uniquely different from the majority of sources available. For example, the recitation produced by the Islamic Audio Studio (IAS) of Shaykh Huthayfi has lower sound quality (in terms of audio fidelity) than alternatives, but stylistically is an interesting recording – part of an ambitious audio collection of recitation. The IAS site, originating as part of the Islamic Centre of Blacksburg, Virginia, additionally contains recordings of recitals made by individual members. One example is a recording of the opening *Sūrat al-Fatīḥa* from the Qur'ān, a short verse which many consider to contain the essence of Islam.[22] Recordings of this kind have a documentary nature, and in a sense present the individual reciter's personal expressions of religious feeling, integrated into the computer-mediated environment.

Such personal recordings are in contrast to recordings made by 'experts', commonly accessible elsewhere online, which may also be available commercially. One site, Islamic Bookstore, has combined the availability of recitations online with the opportunity to purchase 'the complete works' on cassette or CD, offering a 'shopping trolley' and credit-card facility.[23] Thus the site's function can simultaneously be religious, educational and commercial. At times they might evoke emotional reactions and notions of a religious experience. This can emerge in different ways. The writer works adjacent to a small mosque. On occasion, he has downloaded calls to prayer or *adhān* (recorded in Medina and elsewhere), and played the recordings aloud in his office. The office window has been open, and the recording has generated a considerable positive reaction from Muslims gathering for communal prayer below. (The timing of the playing of this recording was accidental on the writer's part, rather than a deliberate aspect of a controlled study!)

Other Qur'ān-related resources on the Internet also extend to scholarly guides, background information, and historical data. These are often incorporated in the general content of websites, as articles, commentaries, speeches and sermons. Many sites emphasize that listening to recitation enhances understanding, and individual ability to recite (as part of prayer), and thus forms part of an Islamic obligation. However, little information is provided on *'ilm al-tajwīd* or the science of recitation.[24]

Information on the Qur'ān also appears on Christian-orientated sites, the implications of which will be further discussed later in this book. For example, the works of John Gilchrist, a South African who has dialogued in a rhetorical fashion with the self-styled Muslim preacher Ahmed Deedat, are available. This collection included a 'scholarly guide' to the Qur'ān's compilation, detailing theories and historical phases of the text's recension. This was cited, if not endorsed, on several Muslim sites. The same may not be true of other works listed on the Answering Islam site.[25]

The majority of the above links refer to 'Sunnī'-orientated sites. Although division of the Muslim world into Sunnī and Shī'a contexts does not demonstrate the complexities of affiliations and understandings of Islam, for the purposes of this overview of source material, the general banner of Shī'a Islam will be utilized. However, as within so-called Sunnī 'orthodoxy', there are many different shades of meaning, and not necessarily agreement, over specific issues and interpretations. Many Shī'a sites have been proactive in creating materials for web use, perhaps reflecting the diaspora of Shī'a communities in the West and the sense of separation from homelands in times of exile. For example, those Shī'a Muslims or their descendants expelled or otherwise detached from Iran both before and after Āyatullāh Khumaynī's revolution were not part of a voluntary migrant community. Their wide international dispersal, and lack of numbers even within Muslim contexts containing Sunnī majorities, has led in some cases to sophisticated networking. This is a pattern reflected throughout Shī'a history, and indeed exile and detachment form part of the traditional literature associated with various Imāms who trace their descent from Shī'a Islam's 'founder' 'Alī bin Abī Ṭālib (discussed in chapter 3). Many Shī'a organizations operate in international contexts, and communicate effectively between continents.

In terms of Shīʿa applications of the Qur'ān, several commentaries reflect specific orientations within Shīʿa world view(s). These sites also incorporate dialogue – and in many cases mutual criticism. The application of the Qur'ān is one area in which there can be common ground, and several Shīʿa sites utilize Qur'ān links (discussed above) from Sunnī-orientated sites. The Al-Islam site is organized by the *Ahlul Bayt* Digital Islamic Library Project (DILP). It is one example demonstrating commonality with Sunnī sites in terms of the information *about* the Qur'ān. At times, there are also subtle indications (in its Qur'ān pages) of the Twelver Shīʿa allegiances of its authors: 'Millions of Muslims read the Qur'an daily. Imām Jaʿfar al-Ṣādiq has said that the minimum daily reading of the Qur'an should be fifty verses or one-fourth of the part, about five minutes reading.'[26] Imām Jaʿfar al-Ṣādiq (d.765) being the sixth Shīʿa Imām, this is a direct reference in the site's Qur'ān pages to Shīʿa practice. In addition, DILP strongly asserts ʿAlī's role as the compiler of the 'definitive' Qur'ān text and the author of its (hidden) commentary, subsequently passed on to the Shīʿa Imāms. This assertion is strongly challenged by Sunnī sources. In addition, a number of the esoteric references in the DILP site *could* be interpreted as alluding to (but not exclusively) specific Shīʿa practices. Under the Qur'ān banner, DILP also incorporates discussions on the implications of geographical and archaeological studies for Qur'ānic interpretation, citing diverse Shīʿa scholars to justify such practices – arguments that would be opposed in many other quarters.[27] DILP also identifies the 'familiarity' issue, in terms of the Qur'ānic recitation: it offers a *tarteel* (fast) recitation of the Qur'ān by Shaykh Abd al-Basit Abd as-Samad, and a *tilawah* (slow) recitation by various reciters.

## 2.3 Alternate Muslim expression in cyberspace

In association with recitations available in Cyber Islamic Environments, one area of perceived difference in terms of Islamic primary sources is in the provision on some websites of 'musical' interpretations and/or expressions of Islam, which can be a significant area of difference within the Islamic world. The nearest equivalent, in a Sunnī context, would be the inclusion of *Nashīds* on some sites; this genre, according to some definitions, extends from sung versions of *aḥādīth* to Ṣūfī Naqshbandī sung prayers, and the music of Yūsuf Islām.[28] Sunnī examples located in cyberspace include the video and sound presentation of 'Subahallah Alhamdulillah', a track by the Malaysian group DiWani. This video features the group praying, and film of the *ḥajj* or major pilgrimage to Mecca. The focus was on Malay pilgrims (*ḥajjis*), and the video also showed the text of the Qur'ān (pages being turned), and images of mosques. The music track incorporates Arabic Islamic phrases.[29]

Other Malay Muslim musicians have a presence on the web – either commercially, or provided by enthusiasts. Academics have also provided sites with recitations and 'Islamic music', including *dhikr* (repetition of Qur'ān-ic phrases or the names of God), poems about Muḥammad, and the music of Nusrat Fateh Ali Khan.[30] Music associated with specific ritualistic practices – such as saints' 'birthdays' – can be located on several sites, and provide a representation of popular religion unavailable elsewhere.[31]

Muslim religious music is also contained in anthropological projects online, notably the BBC Musical Nomad, containing a variety of recordings by professional and non-professional musicians from Kazakhstan, Kyrgyzstan and Uzbekistan. This site offers representation in an under-researched area. Much of the music is 'Ṣūfī' in orientation, and unavailable in other formats, although the material did form part of a BBC World Service documentary series. This comprises part of the depth within Islam-related sites on the Internet and, although not produced directly by Muslim organizations, contains a rich diversity of religious material performed by individual Muslims at grass-roots level. Would this site be defined as a Cyber Islamic Environment, given that its motivation and origins are in marked contrast to the manifestos of certain self-proclaimed Muslim sites?

Given that *suwra, aḥādīth,* prayer and other primary forms of Islamic expression found in cyberspace may be contained in 'musical' forms, it may be useful here to consider briefly the position of music in Islam. The dialogue on the Islamic validity of music has been extensive, especially in those circles seeking to exclude forms of mysticism and esoteric activity. The association of music with Ṣufism has led to certain forms of music being suppressed in some contexts. Former pop musician Cat Stevens, now known as Yūsuf Islām, was markedly reluctant to engage in music for a number of years after his conversion to Islam, but now believes it is a valid genre (based on specific musical forms). A synthesis of pre-conversion and post-conversion music can also be found on a Cat Stevens website, including the song for children 'A is for Allah'.[32] Yūsuf Islām incorporates Qur'ānic phrases, *aḥādīth* and instrumentation based on a Sunnī *sharī'a* model in his contemporary work; he has also endorsed aspects of his pre-conversion corpus, and channels royalties from this work into *ḥalāl* projects.

Opposition to music has also been applied as a means to criticize aspects of Shī'a Islam, in particular against the use of sung prayers. These are associated with certain Shī'a ritual practices, and others incorporate narratives about the Imāms. In terms of their profile on the Internet, several Shī'a sites provide such recitations in a variety of languages – including Arabic and Urdu. These are often listed alongside certain prayers, which would be seen as 'inappropriate' in certain non-Shī'a circles; they contain references to imāms whose importance is denied by (elements in) Sunnī orthodoxy. Examples include *nohas* and *mersias* on the Midwest Association of Shī'a Organized Muslims (MASOM) site, on the subject of Karbalā (the site of Al-Ḥusayn ibn 'Alī's martyrdom in 680) and 'Ashūrā (the anniversary day of Ḥusayn's martyrdom). This subject has significance in the Shī'a calendar, and is a sensitive one for the majority of non-Shī'a Muslims, because Ḥusayn was martyred in battle with an Umayyad force. Whilst the religious nature of the Umayyad caliphate is disputed, certain perspectives might define it as a Sunnī force. Recitations on this subject matter could be described as innovations in Sunnī contexts, although, given that Ḥusayn was a descendant of Muḥammad, respect for Ḥusayn's actions can be found in other Sunnī sources, including in Cyber Islamic Environments.

Recitations form part of individual authors' webpages: the Shī'a Muslim Salams site also offers recordings of *salams*, *nohas* and *mersias* performed by the web author. These sources are described as: 'Shī'a Muslim religious hymns that are recited at majlises [mosques] and other religious functions.'[33] The hymns include two high audio-quality sound files, in Urdu, and a listing of these hymns in alphabetical and calendar order (the latter indicates the appropriate hymns and prayers for specific occasions on the Shī'a calendar).[34] Transliterated lyrics of particular *mersias* are provided without translation, perhaps as a resource for other Urdu speakers (given that Urdu text is not provided). Urdu-speaking Shī'a Muslims, primarily in Pakistan, India, and in the diaspora, may believe that, in their minority position, cyberspace is an environment in which religious, cultural and sectarian differences can be articulated with greater safety.

The implications of sound files containing popular religious expression based within Cyber Islamic Environments is significant, especially recitations or expressions containing portions of the Qur'ān, but also those of other important Islamic sources. They provide one indication of diversity of Muslim expression, and are a dimension that is likely to expand in the future, incorporating video material, improved sound quality and faster download times.

## 2.4 Primary sources online

In terms of other Islamic primary sources available in cyberspace, sources representing the sayings and actions of Muḥammad (*aḥādīth* and *sunna*) are well represented. These sources can be accessed through searchable indices, for example, at the USC Muslim Students Association Islamic Server. This offers an effective means of utilizing the *aḥādīth* collections of Muḥammad ibn Ismā'īl Bukhārī, Muslim ibn al-Ḥajjāj, Abū-Da'ūd and Mālik ibn Anas, acknowledged as central Sunnī sources (for those Sunnī Muslims who refer to *aḥādīth*).[35] All four databases can be searched simultaneously for key words and phrases, which is useful for comparative purposes. A search for the key term *ḥajj* provided hundreds of reference possibilities in seconds, although clearly the more specific search parameters are, the more viable a search mechanism like this can be.[36]

A number of significant Sunnī and Shī'a texts are available online. These sources are secondary compared with the Qur'ān, but still retain a significance to many Muslims. They comprise an important component within the analysis of *sharī'a* and the day-to-day life of practising Muslims. Now that Qur'ān sources are well represented online, greater attention is being paid to the digitization of other materials. In terms of representation of primary source material, it is envisaged that many more works in the areas of commentaries (*tafsīr*), *aḥādīth* and Islamic jurisprudence (*fiqh*) will become available from diverse perspectives, presented in a variety of formats. Material is already available in audio form, but several platforms intend to integrate more material in video format onto their sites in the future.

Cyber Islamic Environments have many applications in the sphere of legalistic interpretation, given the computer's ability to search documents rapidly. This assumes that documents have been inputted appropriately and without error, and taken from reliable sources. This is specifically important in terms of materials related to the various *madhāhab* or schools of Islamic law. The use of web-browsers could rapidly identify a portion or portions of jurisprudence, which might then be compared with other sources. Mālik ibn Anas's *Al-Muwatta* (the easy path), referred to above, is one example of a source that became influential in the formation of a specific school of Islamic law, although the term 'school' suggests a rigidity, rather than the fluid and dynamic basis within much of Sunnī interpretation. This source could be utilized with other legally orientated texts available in cyberspace. For example, the work of the thirteenth-century scholar Yahya ibn Sharaf al-Nawawi is summarized and available under the title *Al-Maqasid* (the objectives). This is a hypertext version of a book that made a great impact as a Shāfi'ī text, originally intended as an aid to the memorization of *fiqh* (jurisprudence).[37]

The work of Muḥammad ibn Idrīs al-Shāfi'ī (767–820), the founder of a school of jurisprudence, features on the Internet, frequently in conjunction with promotions for book publications, but also with some of his interpretations. Pages from his most important work, *Al-Risāla* (the sermon), can be located in cyberspace as straight text, without any subject search-engine. At this stage, the related webpages offer information that is widely available in other formats as read-only text, eschewing many of the advantages of online information sources in relation to accessibility.[38]

A juristic primer can also be located in cyberspace, based on the writings of the Andulusian philosopher Abū 'l-Walīd Muḥammad b. Aḥmad Ibn Rushd (1126–98). Basically, this is a reproduction of Ibn Rushd's text *Bidayat al-Mujtahid.* In its online form, the text runs to hundreds of entries in three volumes. Given its European origins (in Islamic Spain), it is interesting to note that this cyberspace version of Ibn Rushd's work is produced in Northern Ireland.[39]

In the related field of Islamic philosophy, few sources can be located online. The writer's several Internet searches on the subject were unsatisfactory. Much of the material available was publicity for book publications on luminaries, such as the commentator on philosophy Abū Ḥāmid Muḥammad al-Ghazālī (1058–1111), rather than hard text. Biographical material based on existing printed sources can also be located online.[40] Namesakes also appear highly on indices. It is imagined that this apparent deficiency in sources is one that might be rectified in the future, but could also indicate that the interests of dominant Islamic pages do not necessarily incorporate one of the most significant (but also controversial) fields in Islamic thought. Perhaps, at present, Muslim philosophical interests may be less 'wired' to the Internet than their theologically centred peers. Issues of inclusion also emerge, when neither 'Islam' nor 'Al-Ghazālī' appear on websites with titles such as 'Philosophy in Cyberspace'.[41]

Shī'a legal diversity, especially in relation to decision-making processes, is also reflected on several sites in cyberspace. In Shī'a Islam, the concept of *ijtihād* (striving for interpretation of primary sources in light of contemporary conditions) can possess a different emphasis from the definition(s) of the term that can be found in Sunnī orthodoxy. Thus, the concept of *fatāwā* or rulings on specific issues has a particular significance, especially in relation to the opinions of specific contemporary *imāms* and *āyatullāhs*. For example, the rulings of Āyatullāh al-Uzma al-Sayyid 'Alī al-Ḥusayni al-Seestani are detailed on webpages containing translations of material gathered from his writings. These cover a wide range of issues, ranging from primary religious issues relating to *ḥajj* and prayer, through to contemporary concerns such as Muslim approaches to credit cards, insurance, copyright, post-mortem and organ donation.[42] The role of the Internet in decision-making frameworks is discussed later in this book.

The availability of Islamic sources on the Internet can be interpreted as one reflection of diversity in Islamic contexts, in terms of the breadth of material available. This can be seen (and heard) through downloading specific recitation files, and copies of Qur'ānic interpretation. However, there is also the theme of *tawḥīd* or unity, in the context of the common application of Qur'ān translations in the Sunnī context. The notion of an electronic *umma* might be incorporated in an understanding that the majority of Cyber Islamic Environments with religious resources pages link into one or more of the Qur'ān websites available online. However, representations of diversity do emerge in discussions on 'legal' issues and interpretative matters.

The cyberspace landscape is one that Muḥammad might recognize, in terms of some sources, but if he were to return, the Prophet would also identify some of the schismatic behaviour that he predicted, and that the Qur'ān reflected upon:

> And verily this Brotherhood of yours is a single Brotherhood and I am your Lord and Cherisher: therefore fear Me (and no other).
>
> But people have cut off their affair (of unity) between them into sects: each party rejoices in that which is with itself.[43]

# 3

# *Muslim diversity online*

## 3.1 Introduction

Cyber Islamic Environments represent one barometer of diversity within the Islamic spectrum. This is indicated to a degree in the different interest sites that have emerged online, network globally with their own members, inform other Muslims of their activities, and/or propagate their message to non-Muslims. These sites range from individual efforts through to important elements within large-budget organizations.

## 3.2 Surfing the Sunnī Islamic spectrum

Sites may describe themselves as Muslim or Islamic, whilst representing a cross-section of concerns. The conceptual framework of Islam, seeking to influence all aspects of human behaviour, is an important one for Muslims. This is reflected to some extent in the types of sites available in cyberspace. The issue of representation has significance, given that not every aspect of Islam maintains an online presence. Certain perspectives may be seen to 'dominate' the Internet, for example, so-called reform-centred opinions associated with specific interpretations focused upon the Qur'ān and Sunna.

The pervasive influence of what could be described as 'neo-Wahhābism', and related organizations such as Jamā'at-i Islāmī (promoted through the writings of Mawdūdī), was found through an examination of primary source material. The term neo-Wahhābism, in this context, is associated with interpretations of Muḥammad Ibn 'Abd al-Wahhāb's teachings (1703–92). His association with ascendant powers in Arabia during the eighteenth century formed a religious foundation upon which, two centuries later, Saudi Arabia was established. Ibn ʿAbd al-Wahhāb was himself influenced by the Ḥanbalī school (*madhhab*), based upon the teachings of Aḥmad ibn Ḥanbal (780–855). This Sunnī school or *madhhab* (in its varying forms and contexts) strictly focuses upon the Qur'ān and Muḥammad's actions and sayings (Sunna), and articulated itself strongly against innovations, including aspects of esoteric Islam and 'speculative' theology.

The Ḥanbalī *madhhab* influenced Ibn Taymiyya (1263–1328), a theologian and legal scholar, whose writings emphasized that independent judgement could be applied when interpreting Islamic primary sources, without necessarily having recourse to legalistic precedent, creating interpretations specific for particular historical or cultural contexts.

This line of reasoning influenced certain subsequent Sunnī reformers and authorities, which in turn played significant roles in the evolution of varied modernizing perspectives in Islamic thought. Certain of these viewpoints are located on the Internet, although definitions of 'reform' and 'modernity' vary considerably. Each site has its own dimensions and understandings, many of which merit in-depth analyses alongside other source material (available in varied media forms).

Defining 'Islam' is a significant question when discussing aspects of 'political Islam', which often cannot be effectively integrated within a single paradigm: '. . . in Islamic political thought, one has to confront the problematic status of political thought in Islam, and one must try to approach it in a way other than by analogy with modern political thought.'[1] This is relevant when approaching 'political' aspects of Islam online, and the sometimes fluid notions of identity: 'Precisely because the symbolism and the language are inherently flexible and even ambiguous, one Muslim's image can be another's "counter image".'[2]

Such inherent flexibility is particularly relevant when exploring Muslim diversity online. For example, extra dimensions of the terms 'reform' and 'modernity' emerge within Ṣūfī contexts, and from various Shīʿa interpretations of Islam, which may have political dimensions. As will be seen, the Internet is additionally being applied as a means to counter dominant Islamic world views online. Alternative viewpoints, especially within the fields of popular religion, have a voice. Traditional perspectives utilize the Internet to promote views that some Muslim surfers might find anachronistic. Minority interpretations of Islam, not always recognized by the mainstream as Islamic, also express themselves vociferously online.

The spiritual focus of Islam is Mecca. It would therefore be natural for an individual surfer, seeking out Cyber Islamic Environments, to direct search-engine enquiries to Mecca. This writer's random search for the word Mecca, utilizing the popular Yahoo! Internet directory, located various high schools (in Mecca in the United States), and the application of the term 'mecca' as a noun describing attractive qualities of various sites. The first twenty matches offered no Muslim sites.[3] The alternate transliterated spelling 'Makkah' linked to various hotel groups in Saudi Arabia, and a commercial site offering a city guide.[4]

Whilst many Cyber Islamic Environments refer to Mecca, at the time of writing, there was no central site. The Yahoo! Country Index contained no entry for Saudi Arabia. Searches for information on Saudi Arabia elicited academic and governmental sites outside the kingdom, including the CIA World Fact Book and the US Army Area Handbook. The majority of information listed came from academic sites, including universities and companies or individuals *outside* Saudi Arabia. This information includes commercial data and cultural information for potential employees. However, Saudi Embassies in London and the United States have established sites, including the Islamic Affairs Department in Washington DC.[5] This offers a breakdown of Sunnī 'orthodoxy', and material reproduced from other propagation sources. This incorporates Khurshid Ahmed's writings: he is a key figure in Jamā'at i-Islāmī and other Muslim platforms, both in Britain and Pakistan, and the director of the World Assembly of Muslim Youth. Other publications on the site are endorsed by Shaykh 'Abd al-Aziz Ibn Baz, a senior Saudi *'ālim* (scholar). None of the material on the site is unique to the net, neither is it particularly accessible to the surfer.

Islamic sites produced *inside* Saudi Arabia were very limited at the time of writing during 1998–9. The Islamic University at Al-Madina and King Saud University both host pages outlining courses. King Faisal Specialist Hospital and the Saudi Arabian National Guard have general pages. However, compared with other Muslim environments, this reflects wider issues of access to the Internet and the lack of available Internet server providers within many cultural contexts.

Aspects of Sunnī 'orthodoxy' are represented on a wide range of sites outside Saudi Arabia. Comprehensive material is located within minority contexts, such as the Belfast Islamic Centre (BIC). This is one of the earliest examples of a dedicated Cyber Islamic Environment operating from the UK, and was founded in November 1995. Run by two volunteers, BIC adapted to changes in technology, and perceives the future in terms of refining services to a more specialized remit, given the logistical complexities of offering information on 'all aspects' of Islam. The initial ambition was:

> to set up the first Internet site hosting the first mosque in the online world. At that time [1995], the Internet was still painfully slow, crude and predominantly text-based. Therefore the choice for this medium was not because of its speed and tech[nical] benefits but rather it was thought that this would become a more popular and increasingly important medium in the future. Naturally, we started our services in publishing and archiving articles, because at that time, none of the obvious advancement that we see in the Internet now (audio/video) could seem feasible then. Eventually, we feel that the services that we offer will become more specialised . . .
>
> Although we were motivated to establish the first mosque on the Internet, we have not concentrated all our efforts to community based service for the Belfast audience (not only due to the fact that few are connected online), but rather most of our efforts have been directed towards a global audience . . .
>
> . . . We do not see ourselves as storing a monotonous view of Islam but instead, we are working towards sharing the many different views and cultures that give Islam its essence and character that we see contemporarily and as important, its traditional setting as well.
>
> We hope to get a wide range of audience, whether Muslims or non-Muslims interested in sophisticated and specialised interest in Islamic related studies and information.[6]

With this global focus, BIC's locally orientated material is restricted to information on mosque activities, prayer times and education:

> The location of Belfast seemed negligible to the content of the site apart from its community based service. This is not due only to the

fact that we do not emphasise local-directed activity but the nature of the Internet seems to be boundless and independent from the location you are in.

From our point of view it is more beneficial for the content of the site to be 'beyond Belfast' as being global includes the local but not otherwise. One tremendous benefit from this, for example, a weekly newsletter for the mosque can be produced simply by just compiling a few articles from the site or *BICNews*. Otherwise, without such a global-input, it would be twice as hard to gather material for the physical newsletter in the local mosque.[7]

The BIC has the advantage of being, developmentally, several years ahead of the competition in digital terms. The Muslim population in Northern Ireland is small (approximately 3,000). Perhaps because of its geographical and psychological isolation, BIC has attempted to represent (within Sunnī parameters) a cross-section of Muslim perspectives and sources operating within a globalized context. The success of this can be seen in the number of hits (or visits) BIC receives, and in the way it continually updates its resources.

BIC archives incorporate the Shaykh ad-Darsh column, originally featured in the Muslim magazine *Q-News*. Darsh, an Egyptian scholar trained in the prestigious Al-Azhar University, addressed a variety of questions on contemporary issues. BIC also additionally provides a daily bulletin of Islam-related news from diverse sources, with over 11,000 e-mail subscribers. Surfers will find that BIC is extensively linked to other Islamic sectors of cyberspace. The organizers have ambitions to extend the service within the boundaries of financial resources and technical knowledge:

Unfortunately, the progress of our site is limited to my technical knowledge, so the lack of fancy animation, multi-media and so on are not due to an undesirability in embracing these new plug-ins. Further progress may need somebody else to develop these areas . . .

Besides, I'm also taking account of the tactical situation with regards to our presentation and 'marketing' tactics – we certainly do not want to make our site too complex with un-navigable frames or that it will take longer time than necessary to download. We are trying our best, and believe that the sensible approach in the 'entangled-world of the web' is to make things simple.

> . . . I sincerely hope that it will positively contribute to a more mature understanding of this culturally rich and diverse religion, [and] we hope that this model will continue well into the next millennium and be copied by other committed persons . . .
>
> One such project is the regular columnist programme, that is intended to give opportunities to young and old writers alike, to encourage and develop potential or able writers in their pursuit of writing contemporary issues (or any other field that they may feel comfortable with) and their skills in analysing and being critical in their approach.
>
> Furthermore, in the future, we plan to popularise neglected subjects such as falsafa [philosophy], the humanity sciences and history, and are hopeful that this will become more useful than the presently superficial source of reference for students, scholars and the common reader alike.[8]

The BIC site is clearly an important one, in developing a balanced approach to the application of Internet resources. Its reach would be comparable (or superior) to any Muslim print publication in the UK. The emphasis on providing information, rather than complex frames or multimedia, enhances accessibility, especially if members of the target audience (as with any target audience) do not necessarily possess state-of-the-art computer equipment. When animation and lurid colour confront the reader, this can also distract from a site's message and ethos.

BIC wishes to develop its own writers, and provide 'publishing' opportunities to those denied by other media. This should be monitored closely, given the current reliance on articles from other (print) sources. The Internet does allow opportunities for writers with the appropriate equipment to 'publish' their thoughts, although whether an Internet surfer chooses to read them is another issue. The provision of a central forum such as BIC is important, given its profile. Editorial control would be of fundamental significance, in order to avoid some of the excesses of other sites.

An example of BIC's work in this area was the reproduction of a conference lecture given by Abdal Hakim Murad entitled 'British and Muslim'.[9] The BIC site might, in part, answer some of the controversial questions relating to identity that Murad raised in his article, in that the Internet provides an opportunity for individuals to assert and define Muslim identity (or identities) in a 'British' context and express that assertion globally. The profile of Muslims in Britain will be influenced by the content of Cyber Islamic Environments such as BIC, accessed by thousands of surfers from a variety of social and cultural contexts.

There is a variety of other Sunnī perspectives on the net, applying extensive resources. An important, separate developmental progression from BIC is Muslims Online, which, as well as providing news and information, endeavours to provide other Internet resources for its users. These include the provision of free e-mail and mailing lists. Muslims Online additionally hosts free webspace, for organizations and individuals to host their own sites within a *ḥalāl* environment:

> Any Muslim association, of any size, in any industry, in any part of the world, can order a WWW [World Wide Web] home page. All an associations [*sic*] need to do is e-mail us a 1,000-word description of their association and logo on a gif format [picture format] on disk and we'll have their home page on the WWW, at *http://www.muslimsonline.com*. We hope all associations will take advantage of this offer.
>
> Associations who set up a home page will be able to immediately advertise their home page. As an added benefit, MOL will put all the association home pages on its own home page, in one large, searchable database. In effect, Muslims Online hopes to create a site where anyone on the Internet can go to find information about any Muslim association. Interested associations should e-mail Muslims Online immediately.
>
> Our goal at Muslims Online is to encourage Muslim organisations and businesses to come online and make use of the Internet medium, inshallah [God willing].[10]

The site hosts 'Muslim Chat', allowing moderated discussion on selected issues for members. In many ways, this (and other sites) could be seen to be emulating the concept of a global *umma*, through facilitating access to ideas and communication without boundaries. A database of interested participants would be useful for Muslim platforms in many other contexts, relating to the rapid spread of opinions and resources. An awareness of the role of the Internet in global contexts is demonstrated in the site's own mission statement:

> Muslims Online is an effort dedicated to promoting the use of the

> Internet within the Muslim Community. With the explosive growth of the Internet being a fairly recent phenomena, we feel it is imperative for Muslims to generate and produce their own content on the World Wide Web. Inshallah [God willing], this site will develop into a central location where Muslims can read content, exchange ideas, and keep abreast of community events. Alhumdulillah [praise be to God], the internet, like the Muslim world has no bounds, and we hope that this new medium will help in uniting and strengthening our ummah by widening the channels of communication between our Muslim brothers and sisters.[11]

This widening of communication channels represents an important facet of the Internet, although the extent of this expansion of boundaries has some limitations. The Muslims Online listing of 'top sites' excludes elements of Islam described as schismatic or deviational by some – such as the Nation of Islam, and *Aḥmadiyah* sites: 'All Islamic sites with authentic content (ex[cept]: no sites of Submitters, Ahmadiyas, NOI [Nation of Islam] etc.) can make this list, but only the ones to offer the most and best Islamic oriented information or services may make it to the Top Ten.'[12] This is not an exclusive characteristic of Muslims Online. Given the breadth of sources available on the Internet, parameters have to be drawn. Ideological differences emerge in cyberspace (as elsewhere), and are articulated in various ways.

According to the strategy of Muslims Online, it would seem that the 'best Islamic oriented information or services' incorporate aspects of Sunnī orthodox idealism. The concept of a single *umma* has its limitations. This is further reinforced in the choice of links to other sites, which include sites focused on (and constructed around) propagation against Aḥmadiyah groups.[13]

A further significant primary navigation route is the Islamic Gateway (IG), utilizing webspace provided from Muslims Online. IG has an emphasis on multimedia resources, and has an international team of twenty people (based in the USA, the UK and Pakistan), including the owner of an Islamic software company. IG also promotes its own CD-ROM, containing material derived from the Internet. IG constantly updated its media selection, which in 1999 included video recordings from Mecca, clips of Malcolm X, and film relating to the Qur'ān, much of it unavailable elsewhere on the Internet. There are also some unusual offerings, including a twenty-one-minute audio file of a prayer performed by Imām Sa'ad Al-Kamidi, during which the reciter breaks down in tears.[14]

The commercial aspects of this IG site, including the link to an American bookstore, might make the site financially self-sustaining. Technically, IG is one of the most proficient Cyber Islamic Environments, with well-designed pages allowing for ease of navigation and download. The IG 'mission statement' is linked with specific values and ideals:

> The main aim of IG is to create an open, independent, non-partisan, non-profit public-access media service with the right-of-reply for all Muslims and Islamic organisations.
>
> With the grace of Allah, the Islamic Gateway has grown in size and support over the years. IG is in the unique position to freely collaborate with other Muslim online and off-line media projects, both non-profit and commercial while maintaining independence from any political or commercial group.
>
> Unlike other Islamic websites IG is NOT run by a single individual or organisation or by a small group of friends from the same university or city. IG is managed by a large number of volunteers from many provinces of the Ummah from different backgrounds yet working together. IG receives guidance, usually when IG requests (infrequently), from a group of Ulema and learned activists (IG patrons) who are all in favour of using media and the net to help Muslims. This ensures community and public accountability. Patrons, on a sharia basis, can overrule or dismiss individuals from IG service.[15]

This interaction between '*ulamā*' (scholars) and the IG team is interesting, especially in terms of community accountability. Unlike BIC, which is operated from a mosque, this is an example of a digitally linked network whose decision-making processes can be influenced directly by (a definition of) *sharī'ā*. This difference is stressed, perhaps as an implicit criticism of other sites.

The issue of representation and a non-partisan web service is relevant when exploring the breadth of material available on the site. This includes the Malcolm X video clip (recorded in his Sunnī phase), and links to politically activist platforms such as Al-Muhājiroun, Supporters of Shariah, and Ḥizb-ut-Ṭahrīr (discussed in chapter 4). There are also some unique websites provided through IG's own free Internet space, notably the 'Ṣūfi Fighting Movie Arts Production'. This site sought to produce an

Islamic martial arts film, and the site's 'pitch' sought investment through a *ḥalāl* model of finance:

> Film is 90 minutes for art action audience. Very fast action filmed in desert and Muslim village, with Islamic instructions and complete educational on stick and blade fighting, Malaysia Filipino style. For costing we need a sponsor at present to donate total of US $5000. But, less is also fine. A group of people can donate US $500 or so, and we will return everybody's money with profit also once we screen the film.[16]

The site also has video clips instructing in various aspects of martial arts, and a tutorial in aspects such as 'Primary Blocking Methods' and 'Twelve Strike Angles with 22 inch rattan Stick'(!).

Other unusual IG-hosted sites include Rashida's Skincare Page, recipes and the Comfort Zone matrimonial service advertising prospective partners and contact details (within Islamic parameters). The IG mission statement theoretically certainly seems broader than some other 'central sites', although there are still areas of ideological exclusion:

> IG's primary aim and objective is to provide the Ummah with an open and independent forum where information and ideas can be presented and exchanged. All Muslims regardless of race, colour, geographical location and belief are welcome to use and contribute to the Islamic Gateway project. The only exception to this is those sects which have been declared outside the Ummah by every Muslim country and group. These sects are the Qadianis (Ahmedis) and [other group]. Islamic Gateway will not support or associate with any group or Internet site associated with these sects. The Islamic Gateway accepts its responsibility as a Muslim site and is active against these sects and supports those groups who work to educate the Ummah about these groups.
>
> Islamic Gateway is an open forum where all legitimate views and Islamic beliefs can be represented. The Islamic Gateway promotes healthy debate and open discussion. All sects and Islamic groups involved in the Islamic Gateway project should accept that an opposing view to their beliefs and ideals will also be represented on the Islamic Gateway. By allowing all to have their say, the Islamic Gateway can uphold its aim of being an open, independent, non-partisan medium for the whole Ummah.[17]

To some readers, there might be an inherent contradiction between these two paragraphs, raising issues of defining terms such as 'independent' and 'non-partisan' whilst at the same time excluding the Qādianī (or Aḥmadiyyas) groups, in a similar way to Muslims Online. The IG site also incorporates substantial criticism of certain *aḥādīth* sources, and opposes aspects of reform articulated by other platforms. These opinions are also reproduced on the CD-ROM.[18] Many other groups and interests do not have a presence at this moment. There may be a combination of ideological and legalistic issues at play here, together with crucial questions associated with identity concerns. Technically, the IG site is at the forefront of Islamic technical development, for example in offering innovative programmes for teaching prayer (CyberSalat), and calculating packages for prayer times and moon sightings which are particularly relevant during the month of Ramaḍān.

The platforms represented above are operating within their formative phases, so it will be interesting to return to them in the future to determine how they have evolved. Prior to an exploration (or navigation) around specific platforms with focused Islamic or Muslim agendas, it is also useful to discuss the representation of Shī'a Islam within its diverse online forms.

## 3.3 Surfing the Shī'a Islamic spectrum

When surfing Shī'a cyberspace, it is helpful to be aware of what distinguishes Shī'ism from other forms of Islam. The Shī'a, literally the 'party' (of 'Alī), can be defined as those Muslims following the interpretations, traditions and spiritual-physical lineage of Muḥammad's son-in-law, 'Alī ibn Abī Ṭālib (*c.* 598–661). The diversity of Shī'a Islam has its roots firmly within the life of 'Alī ibn Abī Ṭālib. He encapsulates the founding virtues of Shī'ism, which subsequent generations of Shī'a Muslims have attempted to follow.

In Islamic biographical and traditional sources, 'Alī's life is closely associated with Muḥammad's, although this proximity has been interpreted in different ways (this is also reflected within Cyber Islamic Environments). To the majority of Sunnī Muslims, 'Alī is a 'Companion' of Muḥammad; to Shī'a Muslims, 'Alī is a Companion *and* the chosen successor to Muḥammad. Shī'a

Muslims generally believe that ‘Alī was thwarted in his ‘chosen’ role of succeeding Muḥammad by the machinations of (some of those within) the circle of the first three successors to Muḥammad: Abū Bakr (573–634), ‘Uthmān b. ‘Affān (d. 656), and ‘Umar b. al-Khattāb (591–644).

These successors, or *khulafa’* (caliphs), were selected by a committee from Mecca, which judged them eligible according to criteria based upon acceptance of the Qur’ān and the sunna, and membership of Muḥammad’s Quraysh tribe. During the process of Islam’s expansion after Muḥammad’s death, certain flaws, administrative problems and military defeats led to suggestions by detractors (including ‘Alī’s supporters) that the caliphs did not deserve their status. When, in 656, ‘Alī did become the fourth *khalīfa* in Kūfa (in contemporary Iraq), he faced serious military opposition in the form of the second caliph’s relative, Mu‘āwiyya ibn Abī Sufyān. ‘Alī’s own alliances weakened, and ultimately he was assassinated in 661. ‘Alī’s second son Ḥusayn b. ‘Alī (626–80) sought to continue in his father’s role. Ḥusayn’s life and subsequent martyrdom in the Battle of Karbalā became further exempla to the Shī‘a.

Traditions and interpretations of Islam based upon the sayings and actions of ‘Alī and his descendants became a foundation for Shī‘a beliefs, in addition to the Divine Revelation within the Qur’ān, and Muḥammad’s *aḥādīth* and sunna. Gradually a separation in Muslim perspectives occurred, between those who attributed an infallible and divine status to ‘Alī (and his descendants), and those *Ahl al-Sunna* (People of Tradition) whose focus was on Muḥammad (and to a lesser extent the first four caliphs, and the early Muslim community).

Both elements hold in common the Qur’ān, and general principles about Islam. However, the Shī‘a believed that a *Mahdī* or ‘rightly guided one’ was prophesied in the Qur’ān to ‘. . . come at the end of time to “fill the world with justice and equity as it is now filled with injustice and oppression” ’.[19] Whilst this is also a Sunnī belief, a significant difference in Shī‘a perspectives was the belief that the *Mahdī* would emerge from the family line of ‘Alī. Until that time, *Imāms* descended through the surviving son of Ḥusayn were to maintain Shī‘a Muslim traditions, provide new judgements upon legal and governmental matters, and interpret previous Muslim thought. The line of *Imāms* became fragmented in Shī'a history, leading to variations in principles and understandings, including the Zaydī, Ithnā 'Asharī and Ismā'īlī branches of Shī'ism.

Elements of this fragmentation can be observed in Cyber Islamic Environments. There are numerous variations in Shī'a belief systems, with offshoots possessing diverse loyalties and features. These may incorporate their own particular structures and institutions of government. Earthly power ultimately rests with the Imām, a term which can possess connotations in Shī'a beliefs relating to spiritual (and socio-political) leadership.

It can be useful to separate the ideals of Shī'a 'theocracy' from historical, religious and political realities, especially when examining these aspects on the Internet. Many of the events surrounding 'Alī, Ḥusayn, and their descendants are played out through various Shī'a ritualistic expressions, and additionally have a place online. Issues associated with Shī'a beliefs are frequently articulated (and argued) within and between Cyber Islamic Environments. Dispersal and movement of Shī'i Muslim people over the centuries mean that pockets of Shī'ism are located within diverse global contexts. Numerous aspects of Shī'ism are 'wired' into the net, including elements that are not necessarily shared with 'Sunnī' Muslims. Networks of communication rely upon electronic media, for example in the area of decision-making processes.

Given this diversity, locating an 'entry point' to Shī'a beliefs within Cyber Islamic Environments can be difficult. If one were to undertake a search for 'Alī ibn Abi Ṭālib, sites emerge both from Sunnī and Shī'a perspectives. The Saudi-backed platform World Association of Muslim Youth (WAMY), for example, presents a 'Sunnī' interpretation of 'Alī – negating previously discussed Shī'a interpretative perspectives.[20]

One effective site, from a Shī'a perspective, is Al-Islam. This is linked to the organization whose name derives from *Ahl ul Bayt* (People of Muḥammad's House), and contains detailed files in various formats on aspects of Shī'ism, ranging from the life of Muḥammad through to the Twelfth Imām (and 'beyond'). A significant proportion of the material is in the form of articles, although there are also sound files and other multimedia – including lectures in Urdu, Gujurati, Arabic, English and Persian on subjects such as martyrdom and the destruction of Shī'a shrines. There is an extensive sound archive, highlighting the specific phenomenological aspects of Shīʿa Islam distinguishing it from Sunnī belief. This includes an alternative *adhān* (call to prayer), and specific prayers relating to ʿAlī ibn Abī Ṭalib and other members of his family (and descendants).[21]

A number of specific perspectives within the Shīʿa spectrum are represented online, although limited material exists on some branches. For example, the majority of searches on *Zaydī* Shīʿism elicit only basic information on Yemen – where the majority of Zaydīs are located. Zaydīs were perhaps the first significant division in Shīʿism, founded in 900, and revering ʿAlī's line emanating from the fifth Caliph Imām Zayd ibn ʿAlī (d. 740). Very little Internet information on Zaydīs is produced in Yemen itself. The CIA World Factbook, academic sites and expatriates dominated this sector of Shīʿa Islamic cyberspace.[22]

This can be compared with Ismāʿīlī sites: the Ismāʿīlī branch of Shīʿa Islam is associated with one of the successors of the Sixth Imam, Jaʿfar al-Ṣādiq (*c.* 765). A dispute meant that one group followed Jaʿfar's son Ismāʿīl. This Ismāʿīlī line itself fragmented at subsequent intervals, forming disparate branches including the Fāṭimids, the Nizāris, the Assassins, Bohorās and the followers of Aghā Khān. Ismāʿīlī communities have several sites linked into the Ismāʿīlī Web. This is a multimedia site, regularly updated with information about the Ismāʿīlī leader, the Aghā Khān, and also networking the community through link pages, including a site for Ismāʿīlī children.[23]

A principal development in Shīʿa thought was the 'Occultation' or disappearance of the Twelfth Imām, Muḥammad b. al-Ḥasan al-ʿAskarī (al-Qāʿim) (869–940), who it was anticipated would return as *al-Mahdī* to lead the Shīʿa community. Followers of this branch of Shīʿa Islam (and related offshoots) are known as *Ithnā ʿAsharī*s or 'Twelvers', and include the majority of Iran's Shīʿa Muslim population, together with a significant proportion of Iraq's Muslims.

Websites containing Twelver Shīʿa material frequently incorporate perspectives associated with contemporary Iran, both in support of and in opposition to the government's ideology. A number of sites feature information on Āyatullāh Rūḥullāh Khumaynī (1902–89), the Imām or spiritual leader whose revolution paved the way for the introduction of a theocratic governmental system in Iran in 1978. In 1998, the Iranian government launched the Sun's House, a website based at the Imam Khomeini Cultural Institute's International Affairs Division.[24] The Sun's House received the endorsement of Khumaynī's grandson (as discussed in the Introduction). The site's intention is to place Khumaynī's complete works online. Material already published includes selected sayings and biographical material related to the Imām, together with video clips from a variety of sources – such as western media film from the time of the revolution. The Photo Album incorporates family snapshots of an informal nature that contradicts many of the austere official media images of Khumaynī.[25] The archive contains photos of his exile, and powerful images of his return to Iran have a strong historical interest.

The Sun's House connection with the IRNA (Iranian Republic News Agency) provides access to film media representing Khumaynī's life, that attempts, in the words of the films' presenter, to contradict hostile western perceptions of Khumaynī. Video clips of several minutes' duration demonstrate different aspects of the Imām. Archive film includes what is described as Khumaynī's 'Ascension' (essentially film of his funeral). Video showing his 'home' (burial place), which is now a shrine at Behesht-e-Zahra in Tehran, provides documentary material difficult to obtain elsewhere (aside from a personal visit).[26] Certain Muslim perspectives believe that praying at shrines or at tombs is inappropriate, so this representation is one which other dimensions in Cyber Islamic Environments might disagree with, even if they supported the ethos behind the revolution, and the stimulus it provided in other contexts.

Topics on the Sun's House centre on aspects of Khumaynī's interpretation of Shīʿa Islam, from works such as 'Theology and Servitude' through to Khumaynī's explanation of *Jihad-e-Sazandegi* (Crusade for Reconstruction). The extensive multimedia facets of the Sun's House demonstrate awareness of this technology's *daʿwa* (propagation) potential, through disseminating Khumaynī's perspectives. The site is central to the IRNA (and therefore governmental) strategy to promote Khumaynī's particular understanding of Shīʿa Islam, mirrored (to an extent) in a Farsi version of the site.[27] However, the Internet has been heavily criticized by certain elements in the Iranian clergy, who have accused it of 'corrupting Iranian society'.[28] It remains to be seen whether, in the long term, the Sun's House will temper that criticism:

> Correspondents say official attitudes inside Iran to the Internet are ambiguous. The traditionalist Shiite Muslim clergy is fiercely opposed to the Internet that it fears will allow Western cultural influence into the Islamic republic. But the Iranian government runs Websites for its own statements and for Shiite religious material. The service is available to the public, but access is restricted by high costs.[29]

This issue of access is also reflected in (Muslim and other) contexts. The extent to which external sites can be filtered out is very limited. In the future, the ability of authorities to place restrictions on accessing Internet sites *may* become even more difficult, given developments which will create alternative access to the Internet, for example through satellite links or digital television, and utilizing media other than computers (such as digital telephones).

Sites presenting perspectives on Khumaynī authored by sympathizers outside Iran include the Islamic Centre of England (London) (*sic*). Further photographs, biographical data and multimedia in various formats are provided: the section of 'art' features paintings from the post-revolutionary period. The site also includes data on Āyatullāh al-Oḍma Khamene'ī, the 'spiritual leader' of Iran, and successor to Khumaynī: material includes a sermon, biographical information and the 'rules' of *ḥajj* (in English and Arabic).[30] Since being placed online in 1997, the site claimed to have had over 17,500 hits, suggesting an extensive audience for, or curiosity about, this material.[31] The site maintains a prominent presence on relevant Islam search-engines.

Another website presenting material on Khumaynī is the United Muslims of America, operating at the www.khomeini.com URL (Uniform Resource Locator). This site makes extensive use of its own internal search-engines, facilitating rapid access to material about Khumaynī. This includes an exposition on the 'Forty Hadith', a detailed exegesis, which provides a further understanding of Khumaynī's approaches to Islamic interpretation.[32] Although this work is available in print, the Internet provides Khumaynī's corpus with another avenue for globalized expression, transcending traditional barriers, and potentially increasing the influence of his interpretative perspective. It demonstrates Khumaynī's background in scholarship and academic argumentation, centred in theological institutions in Iran. The interface is very important, as is the 'branding' of the site. Also of interest is how the United Muslims of America site is linked to the Islamic Centre of England, indicating a creative application of (and strategy towards) 'interesting' site names guaranteed to project an air of authority, and promote the curiosity of the casual surfer.

Khumaynī's spiritual successor, Āyatullāh Khamene'ī, is closely affiliated with the Qom Theological Centre, an institute established by Khumaynī in his home city after the Islamic revolution. The Centre has established its own website, directed by Āyatullāh Moḥammad Taqī Miṣbah Yazdī.[33] This site incorporates an index of the institute's publication *Ma'rifat*, a term which relates to esoteric knowledge within Islam (gnosis). *Ma'rifat* includes cover art and abstracts of articles demonstrating perspectives associated with Qom. Subjects include 'The Decline of Moral Standards in the Western Society', 'Islamic Gnosis and Wisdom', 'Clerics, Clerics' Life-style and Development', 'Religious Pluralism in Muslim Thought', and translations of western philosophical theory such as 'Structure and Structuralism' by Raymond Boudon and François Bourricaud.[34] This promotes the ethos of the institute, and implicitly that of Āyatullāh Khamene'ī himself, suggesting endorsement of the Internet from the spiritual head of the country.

The Qom Seminary is significant in terms of the development of Islamic Internet resources. Grand Āyatullāh Moḥammed Reza Golpāygāni, a senior cleric and head of the seminary, endorsed the application of computers in Islam in 1996. This supported a programme to facilitate the development of a research database, containing 5,000 important texts. Its instigator, 'Alī Kuranī, noted:

> 'At first the old clergy thought they were being replaced,' Kurani says. 'You want a computer to issue fatwas [Islamic decrees] instead of us?' they asked. But when they saw the result they were happy. Now they come to do research. They don't know about computers, but they know how to press buttons.[35]

The relevance of the Internet to elements of the clergy in Iran is an important development, and could be contrasted with that of their peers in other locations. Questions need to be asked as to how ideological differences influence or conflict with the introduction of Islamic Internet resources. Apart from the enthusiastic responses detailed in this book, there are also examples of the grudging acceptance of the Internet and its application by others, linked with issues of globalization and the changing nature of religious authority.

The question of 'control' is integral to the process of web development within certain political settings. This is particularly relevant, when there are concerns about opposition groups outside the conventional boundaries of control. This is true in relation to Iran: locating opposition groups online produced *within* Iran raises difficulties. However, *outside* Iran there are several highly developed platforms, with varying levels of religious content. Some have a strong Shī'a religious orientation, acting as a protest platform against current government activities suppressing particular religious perspectives in Iran. For example, the Islam-Iran site includes documentation in Arabic, Persian and English from organizations such as the (self-styled) Council of Shī'a Muslims and the Muslim Council of Friday Imams, protesting against the imprisonment of theologians in Qom and Tehran.[36] It lists the scholars, and seeks to mobilize international Shī'a opinion against the treatment the prisoners are receiving.

The Council of Shī'a Muslims site also links to the human rights group Amnesty International (which itself has been criticized by other Muslim 'authorities'). Documentation in Persian and Arabic includes material endorsing opposition religious leaders, such as Grand Āyatullāh Sayyed Muḥammed Shirazi and Grand Āyatullāh Sayyed Sāḍīq Rawhanī. These interests are reflected in many other sites, from organizations and individuals, especially in the United States. Opposition also comprises supporters of the former regime of the Shah (and advocates of his descendants), such as the Constitutionalists Movement of Iran, who may oppose all religious factions in the contemporary Iranian theological hierarchy.[37]

In relation to the revolution and its ideological shaping, information can also be found on 'Alī Sharī'atī (1933–77), a sociologist whose broad appeal was related to his desire 'to be a politico-religious thinker in the context of the Third World liberation struggles'.[38] The 'Official 'Alī Sharī'atī site' includes

Persian and English text, an archive of audio files containing recordings of various speeches by Sharī'atī, and biographical information. A collection of Sharī'atī writings provides an introduction to his conceptual framework and approach to Islam. This material is not widely available in English, so the opportunity to download entire books (or extracts) of translated and original material may be useful to observers and scholars, as an introductory resource.[39]

Significant areas of Shī'a thought outside Iran include Arab Shī'a perspectives, in locations such as Bahrain, Lebanon and Iraq.[40] Iraq has a substantial majority population of Shī'a Muslims, in particular in the southern region.[41] Important Shī'a shrines are also located in the area. Amongst the contemporary perspectives on Shī'a Islam to have emerged from Iraq, that of Āyatullāh al-Khoei (d. 1992) is significant for many, both in Iraq and in exile. Given limited information channels, and the targeting of Shī'a Muslims by Saddam Hussein, the Internet provides a useful channel for communication.

According to his followers, Āyatullāh al-Khoei was qualified to issue opinions and decisions based on his interpretation of the Qur'ān, and other Islamic sources. Al-Khoei made pronouncements on a number of important contemporary issues, and other 'authorities' endorsed his view. Many of his opinions have been published in print form, and gradually material is now appearing online. Resources on al-Khoei include a full biography, issued through the extensive Al-Islam site – indicating his status as an Imām. The persecution that he suffered under Saddam Hussein is documented.[42] The Al-Khoei Foundation also provides particular interpretations of Shī'a understandings, such as practices associated with the persecution of Ḥusayn ibn 'Alī Ṭalib.[43] A related site based around the work and juristic decision-making of his 'successor' Āyatullāh al-Seestani (b. 1930) contains extensive archives on this particular approach to Shī'a Islam.[44]

The networking of Muslim Shī'a communities in minority contexts is a significant factor in the utilization of Internet resources. Sunnī Muslims often form the majority in a Muslim community. Shī'a Muslims numerically can be dominated, and not necessarily highly regarded, by their Sunnī neighbours (the sentiment may be mutual). An example of this are the Khoja

Shī'a Ithnā 'Asharīs, who are *also* a minority within Ithnā 'Asharī Shī'ism, and indeed Khoja Shī'ism as well. This position has led to persecution, and influenced the dispersal of Khoja Shī'a Ithnā 'Asharīs communities in the Indian subcontinent, east Africa, western Europe and North America. As a means to disseminate information such as religious opinions, or to co-ordinate activities, the World Federation of Khoja Shī'a Ithnā 'Asharīs are utilizing the Internet as a communication resource; they have developed an ambitious framework linking Ithnā 'Asharīs globally.[45] This site is regularly updated, linking different regions together: for example, a survey of death notices included deceased individuals from Los Angeles, Dubai, Nairobi, Karachi, Toronto, Botswana, Romania, Dar-es-Salaam, Seattle, Tehran and London. Invitations to send prayers and condolences by e-mail were included in the notices.[46]

The site also includes business pages: the commercial ethos of many Khoja Shī'a Ithnā 'Asharīs in exile would encourage business networking both within a national and international context. There is a direct link to a self-help European business network known as JIBA (Jaffri International Business Association), comprising well-placed Khoja Shī'a Ithnā 'Asharī business people who seek to support their communities through seminars, advice and information dissemination. According to the chair of JIBA, the organization is a response to global recession, and would appear to contain a religious subtext:

> There is, therefore, created a society replete with frustration and aggression. There is an increased incidence of violence and crime, more marriages and families are splitting up, there is more illness and more depression. These problems are rife all over the world and are not confined to just one nation. The ailing economic state has affected human beings adversely not only financially, but, socially, medically, psychologically and even spiritually.[47]

The networking between Khoja Shī'a Ithnā 'Asharī communities should not disguise the differences within and between communities operating in different social, geographical and cultural contexts. To an extent, this can be evaluated online, by reading the different journals published on the Internet. The Federation of Khoja Shī'a Ithnā 'Asharī Jamaats of Africa publish a regular journal, and include accounts of younger members interacting with their Californian peers. The journal's August 1998 cover offered 'Why the African Federation said YES to compulsory pre-marital HIV or AIDS testing', and links to a detailed account of the issues surrounding HIV in Khoja Shī'a Ithnā 'Asharī communities globally. This is an issue that is under-represented in other Cyber Islamic Environments. The article advises:

> The Islamic life style – chastity before and fidelity within a marriage – is a safeguard against acquiring this disease. Live within the bounds of The Islamic Shariah and adhere to the injunctions prohibiting homosexuality and extramarital sexual relations. Despite the alarming aspects of this illness it is reassuring to know that we have the ability to choose to avoid AIDS and the answer lies in 'living within the precincts of the moral code' as prescribed by Islam and upholding the values of chastity and morality. Being faithful to ones [*sic*] wife or husband is the best way of prevention.[48]

In recognition that this lifestyle may not always be adhered to, the second point on the listing notes: 'If you use a condom use it correctly. Use water based lubricant gel with the condom. Oil based gel can weaken the rubber.' Such statements are not typical in Cyber Islamic Environments for a number of reasons, primarily associated with frequent (but not universal) Muslim antipathy to contraception. The site centres on assumptions of heterosexuality amongst the community. Discussions on the issue of HIV and AIDS reflect concerns voiced in the Khoja Shī'a Ithnā 'Asharī community in London, which the writer observed during fieldwork.[49] Such information could also be accessed in confidence on the Internet. The website additionally addresses more mundane concerns, together with legal *fiqh* interpretations, and photographs of activities. As a representation of this specific Shī'a community and its concerns, the site provides an illuminating overview.

Other aspects of Shī'a beliefs and perspective can be located in Cyber Islamic Environments. Whilst not a substitute for personal interaction or community participation, they provide a foundation for networking and informing relatively small communities, and an avenue for non-Shī'a individuals to learn more about these particular religious perspectives.

## 3.4 Surfing Ṣūfī cyberspace

As well as the 'branches' of Sunnī and Shī'a Islam (and their offshoots) discussed above, other indications of Muslim diversity can be located online. Certain groups or individuals might not identify some of these as Islamic: these include aspects of esoteric Islam associated with Ṣūfism or *taṣawwuf*. This is a broad concept, and numerous *ṭarīqa* Ṣūfī orders exist, with different understandings and conceptual frameworks.

The mystical quest forms part of the Islamic Internet landscape. This can provide an outlet for otherwise marginalized groups, as well as mainstream Muslim popular expression of religious beliefs. The central focus around an individual or an order can provide a different emphasis to other Islamic sites on the Internet. The distribution of texts and propagation material digitally can be effective and comprehensive, and organizations take advantage, either officially or unofficially, of the Internet's networking potential. Like other shades of the Islamic spectrum, Ṣūfis attempt to represent their perspectives online to other Muslims and non-Muslims.

Ṣūfism contains elements of secrecy in some contexts, and historically certain knowledge has been hidden from non-adherents, both because of its mystical qualities, and for fear of persecution as unbelievers straying from conventional Islam. To an extent, these fears are also present today in some contemporary Ṣūfī understandings and practices: however, elements of the esoteric can be located within so-called 'orthodoxy' and with aspects of Shī'ism, and some commentators would suggest that there is a thin line (or common ground) between these practices and Ṣūfism. It has to be recognized that there is not necessarily mutual agreement between *ṭarīqa* orders as to what is acceptable in Ṣūfī practices. Occasionally, these discussions on issues of acceptability appear in Cyber Islamic Environments.

Whilst some Ṣūfī orders may adhere to their practice of dissimulation, others display extensive information relating to allegiances and instructions for believers. For example, the Chishti Habibi Soofie Islamic Order International (Durban, South Africa) provides a breakdown of their interpretation of a *ṭarīqa*, including definitions and perspectives relating to key concepts of beliefs. Terminology is explained, including the allegiances to a *shaykh* or leader of a *ṭarīqa*, and what the benefits of such allegiance can be. It would be useful to consider the role between a *murīd* (follower) and a *shaykh*, especially if that relationship is (or can be) computer-mediated. Specific aspects of belief, including the following of 'saints' and practices surrounding them, are included on the site: many of these details would be seen as 'un-Islamic' in other circles. The Soofie Islamic Order International is not averse to criticizing other orders, extensively detailing what it describes as 'pseudo-Ṣūfism':

> The (false) sufi is busy deceiving men and women;
> The ignorant is busy building his body;
> The wise man is busy with the coquetry of words;
> The lover of Allah is busy with annihilating himself.[50]

The information contained on this site suggests that it offers one strategy for combating this 'pseudo-Ṣūfism'. In order to preserve the order's integrity, the site is proactive in its Internet provision: it offers an e-mail facility for advice, has detailed information on *shaykh*s, and is developing an archive of sermons. The webpages also provide resources that network to other related institutions within this order, in South Africa and India.[51] Like the Khoja Shī'a Ithnā 'Asharī, the Chishti Habibi Soofie Islamic Order International have developed the foundations for electronic interaction and information provision, and operate in a minority context.

The Naqshbandī Ṣufi Way is another example of *taṣawwuf* online, with elements combining specific practices with net technology: a *bay'ā* or pledge of allegiance to the *ṭarīqa* can be heard through clicking of the cursor on the 'hands' of *ṭarīqa* followers represented in a photograph.[52] The American mission of Shaykh Hisham Kabbanī motivated the website, which describes the order as Naqshbandī-Haqqanī, focused on its Grand Shaykh Muḥammad Nazim al-Haqqanī (b. 1922). Al-Haqqanī's own authority and spiritual line of descent from the previous Grand Shaykh is chronicled on the site.[53]

Extensive details of Naqshbandī practices are contained in this site, including transliterated transcripts of various prayer and *dhikr* (repetition) practices: these can be followed in real time through downloading audio files. Thus, the surfer is able to 'experience' aspects of these Ṣūfī practices, which are also explained and justified. For example, Dhikr in Congregation or *Khatm-ul-Khwajagan*, a weekly ritual that is central to the *ṭarīqa*'s practices, can be followed and downloaded: part of this practice is 'silent', but involves repetition. Another aspect is congregational and participative: the numbers of repetitions of a phrase are provided, together with guidelines on their pronunciation. They can also be followed on the audio file download. Shaykh Hisham Kabbani participates directly in the recordings, and can be viewed on film practising *dhikr*. Questions emerge as to whether this could constitute a religious experience for members of the *ṭarīqa* unable to attend a *Khatm-ul-Khwajagan*.[54] It might also contribute to the sense of community, or indeed suggest a digital *umma*, at least for adherents of the order.

The Naqshbandī Ṣufi Way additionally details other practices and concepts specific to the order, illustrated with sound files, including seclusion (*khalwat*), and spiritual exercises. Various levels and spiritual requirements for adherents are incorporated in the site. Practices surrounding *mawlid* – which in this context relates to celebrations of Muḥammad's birthday – are extensively justified.[55] The practices themselves are detailed in Arabic manuscript form, accompanied by over twenty audio files containing recitations and prayers in Arabic performed by the Royal Malaysian Naqshbandi Group.[56]

It must be noted that such practices are not universally endorsed in other elements of the Islamic spectrum. This is made clear, given that the site links into a related Ottoman Muslim site produced by Naqshbandī authors. This articulates and promotes what the authors describe as a 'People of the Sunna' position in relation to Wahhābī doctrine.[57] The entomology of the discussion is complex, with both positions claiming to be descendants of the *Salaf* or 'pious ancestors'. *Salafiyya* has been elsewhere applied in association with various reform-centred perspectives, and also in relation to the Wahhābī perspective promoted in the eighteenth century, ultimately influencing contemporary Saudi religious thought and that of associated reform movements and organizations. Given the position of many websites *against* Ṣūfism, it is perhaps understandable that Ṣūfī sites such as the Naqshbandī devote resources to denounce (anti-Ṣūfī) 'Wahhābīsm'.

Other orders also have a presence online, frequently making use of animation and Internet design to produce an attractive final product. A good example of this is the Attasia Ṭarīkah, associated with its founder 'Abdullah Bin 'Alawī Bin Hassan Al-'Aṭṭas, born in western Java, Indonesia, to a Hadhramatī (Yemeni) family. The Attasia site details the foundation of the order, its attributes, history, and practices. This includes the appointment of leaders at local and 'supreme' levels, including male and female *khulafā'* in the order's mosques in Yemen. This gives a fascinating insight into every aspect of *ṭarīqa* organization, a transparency that is not necessarily reflected elsewhere in Ṣūfī orders. The fact that the web authors placed this material online suggests that there are web-literate Ṣūfīs interested in such minutiae of detail. The site also provides information on how communities meet at their mosques or *zāwiya*, when invited by their local *Khalīfa* for ritual practices. Specific practices instituted by the *ṭarīqa* founder (adapted from traditional Sunnī rituals) are detailed on the website, including a specific festival based on fasting, during six days of the month of Shāwal (in the Islamic calendar).

This practice might be deemed inappropriate or innovative by some Muslim perspectives outside the *ṭarīqa*. The site includes photographs of documents, mosques and religious leaders. The global aspect of the order is represented with images from the Myanmar (Burma) branch. The essence of the order's activities is encapsulated in the audio files provided, including recitations featuring the voice of the Second Supreme *Khalīfa*. The site also incorporates Arabic information which follows a similar format and content to the English-language version of the site, together with documentation on the order, including a *qasīda* or pledge of allegiance.[58]

The Attasia site has multiple applications. As a resource for practitioners, it may provide information in English and Arabic unavailable elsewhere. For Muslims who are not members of this order, it provides an insight into their activities, although they would not necessarily be 'approved' by all. It is also a helpful resource for academics and researchers seeking information on an element of Islam under-represented in sources elsewhere.

Other orders acquired a presence online during 1999. These include pages devoted to regional Ṣūfī interests, areas under-represented on the Internet. The Samaniyya Ṭarīqa, followers of the Sudanese religious leader Shaykh Babiker (d. 1996), established pages 'devoted to his soul', produced in Khartoum.[59] This is particularly relevant, given the opinions about the Internet expressed by other authorities in Sudan – discussed elsewhere in this book.

The issue of endorsement is an important one in Cyber Islamic Environments. Many sites are produced by individual members of orders or sects, and not necessarily endorsed by a *ṭarīqa shaykh*. Such endorsement is not essential, especially given the esoteric nature of various mystical hierarchies. For example, a site detailing several aspects of Ṣūfīsm and its relation to Islamic sources represented the Chistiyya Qādhiriyya order, founded in the thirteenth century in India. This site presents translations of a Shaykh's address to *saliks* (seekers of God), the order's opinions on forms of *shirk* (idolatry), and a detailed esoteric exposition on one form of the Ṣūfī *kalīma* (proclamation of faith). As with other sites, determining (if it is necessary or relevant) whether this is an 'official' site or not is difficult. The site is produced by a Chishti Qādhiriyya follower (and computer programmer) based in Tamilnadu, India. He discussed his own beliefs and inspiration on the site, including what led him into this particular interpretation of Islam. This is one of several Ṣūfī websites produced at grassroots level, within the home environment of an order. The guest book of the site suggests that the reaction to this particular site from other Ṣūfī surfers has been positive. Visitors from the USA, Pakistan, Malaysia and Singapore all left glowing endorsements, suggesting that this site was an important addition to 'Ṣūfī cyberspace':

> I have been searching for a site like yours. A site of a true seeker, a genuine disciple of Sufism. I have seen other sufi sites. But they are rather cold, and unlike yours they are not personal, rather just quoting from here and there. Not at all intimate. As a fellow seeker, of a different path, I know it is important to appreciate the beautiful relationship between the master (or sheikh) and the disciple (murid). And the mystical experiences that happen in the transferring of the flame. I thank you.

> Bismilahhirrahmanirrahim Assalamualikum, Brother Shahul Hameed Faizee, Your work for the cause to spread the 'Chishti Qadiria Order' through this the medium will be well received by all those who wish to seek the truth of 'Tauhid' and I am sure this will be achieved by the

> blessings of our Prophet Muhammad Rasullah Sallallah Alaihi Wassalam and also from your sheik. A magnificent work, deserved to be praised. Well done and I sincerely believe that this website will become one of the most recognized sites in the world. Wasslam.[60]

This unofficial site can be compared with the 'official' Chistiyya site, Dar ul-Iman (Land of Faith), produced in the United States. The content incorporates a breakdown of *raka'āt* prayer sequences and positions, to be applied in consolidation with an instructional sound file commentary on the methodology of prayer. The physiological benefits of prayer are detailed. For example, in the discussion of the *sajjda* position, the following information is imparted:

> Beneficial Effects: The posture of supreme submission and humility. Knees forming a right angle allow stomach muscles to be developed and prevents growth of flabbiness in mid-section; even greater flow of blood into upper regions of body especially the head, including eyes, ears, nose and lungs; allows mental toxins to be cleansed by blood. Excellent effect to maintain proper position of fetus in pregnant women; reduces high blood pressure. Increases elasticity of joints. Annihilates egotism and vanity. Increases patience and reliance upon God. Increases spiritual stations and produces high psychic energy throughout body. It is the essence of worship.[61]

The site provides detailed information on other aspects of esoteric Islam, focusing on the perceived healing benefits of various Ṣūfī practices. These include the role of breath and breathing practices, which are seen to possess a spiritual dimension.[62] The medical and health information continues in other topics, such as 'Foods of the Prophet' and healing 'for the body . . . for the mind or emotions, and . . . for the soul'.[63] Many of these practices might seem outside the realm of orthodoxy, although to some observers they may resemble aspects of New Age beliefs.[64]

The two Chistiyya sites demonstrate different perspectives and areas of interest *within* an order, and are produced in western and eastern contexts. Yet there is interconnectivity between them (as well as a hyperlink!), with shared areas of spiritual concern. The American-based site acts as a 'bazaar' for related products, including CD recordings, health goods and perfumes, which can be purchased online.

Globalization features strongly in Ṣūfī networks. A good example is that of the Tijāniyya order, which is represented online by a branch with strong links in Senegal and the United States. The site discusses the order's founder, Algerian-born Aḥmad al-Tijānī (1737–1815), and his religious experiences, including details of a prophetic vision of Muḥammad. The integral role of Shaykh Ibrahim Niasse (1900–75) in promoting the order in Senegal is eulogized, including his 'reformation' of the order to encourage the education of women. The site extols the virtues of the branch's current leader, Shaykh Hassan Cisse (1945–), who has followers in the United States and West Africa. The Shaykh founded the African American Islamic Institute, including an educational centre in Senegal, at which American students undertake Islamic Studies, and the order has established a strong presence in several US cities. The site succinctly represents key features of this branch of the Tijāniyya order, and encourages surfers to provide financial assistance in order to promote its activities further. Internet sites can act as a fund-raising tool in Cyber Islamic Environments. On this site, they not only propagate their interpretation of Islam, but also present a positive image of Islam through promoting the humanitarian activities of Shaykh Cisse – including his United Nations recognition.[65]

Other Ṣūfī perspectives are well represented online. One of the most interesting Ṣūfī-related sites is Ḥaji Michael Roland's 'Ṣūfīsm in Indonesia', which offers many aspects of belief and religious experience from a unique regional and spiritual perspective. As well as general background introductory material on Ṣūfīsm, specialized information is also provided: for example, on Ṣūfī Masters of Sumatra, Java, Kalimantan (Borneo) and Sulawesi (Celebes). Information on 'Pilgrimage' is offered, consisting of information and photos of many mosques and tombs. This is an example of a representation of Islam that a number of Muslims would consider outside the 'mainstream'. The site provides a representation of popular religion from an adherent's perspective.[66] To what extent will this site inform casual surfers' perspectives on Islam? Many western 'Ṣūfī' orders, associated in some cases with 'New Age' religions, also have an extensive presence on the Internet. Ṣūfī Order International is one example of this, associated with Pīr-O-Murshīd Ināyat Khān and the Ṣūfī Order of the West.[67]

The Internet landscape with regard to Ṣūfism would certainly suggest a shift away from the Sunnī-centric interpretations of Islam that dominate many contemporary western contexts. Muslim diversity online is a broad issue, which has only been introduced here. Other *ṭarīqa* orders and Ṣūfī concepts need to be explored in terms of their representation, which is very limited at present. The 'hidden', esoteric nature of certain Ṣūfī perspectives may negate the need to create a website; in addition, many orders exist at a popular religious level in environments that do not have significant Internet provision. The future may see the Cyber Islamic Landscapes being more fully represented, to incorporate other aspects of so-called Islamic mysticism in many of its forms, including delineation of particular Muslim exponents of the subject.

# 4

# *Politics, Islam and the Net*

## 4.1 Introduction

Dimensions of political diversity in Cyber Islamic Environments are represented in many websites, from different perspectives and levels of society. These include governmental interpretations of Islam, presented as official Muslim perspectives, in both minority and majority Muslim contexts. Such sites may be associated with presentation of policy, commentary on current affairs, reproduction of governmental publications, central data on Muslim institutions, and the presentation of data for non-Muslims. This material *may* also be intended for audiences outside a specific government's zone of power, the web presenting globalization opportunities transcending conventional networks of communication.

Muslim political parties, in both government and opposition contexts, have identified the Internet as an effective area for investment and development. Web platforms on a particular country may operate both from within and outside its geographical boundaries. This represents a new channel through which to inform supporters of activities, and propagate perspectives to other parties. The Internet has potential as a mobilizing force, particularly if networks are not/cannot be controlled and monitored by a central government.

Speeches (in multimedia formats), policy documents and specific interpretations of Islam justifying political perspectives (and other actions) can be located online. Frequently, these are networked to other platforms operating similar sites on related issues. These sites could have the effect of politicizing individuals and activating opposition outside a particular country, especially when opposition groups are restricted.

As well as government and opposition Muslim political platforms online, other perspectives operating outside these spheres exist in cyberspace. Certain of these might be seen as part of the digital *umma*, networking across borders, and reflecting a globalized interpretation of Islam. The Internet might be the perfect medium in which to express these views, given its networking form, its relative flexibility in terms of operating systems and mobility, and because it is inexpensive in real terms (compared with other propagating mediums) given the *potential* audience for a website. However, placing a website online is perhaps easier than persuading surfers to visit it. Word of mouth is one way in which news about a site can be transmitted; links from other websites can also be influential, given that (as seen in earlier chapters) many Muslim websites are unlikely to promote perspectives that are broadly opposed to their own.

Defining a movement as Islamic introduces particular issues relating to criteria of definition: Islam (and its interpretations) may comprise a component of an organization's or individual's world view, motivation and rhetoric. The integration of politics and religion within Islam represents the perspective of Islam as an integrated way of life encompassing all aspects of human activity. The application of religion as a means of mobilizing individuals and communities towards aims that have diverse levels and applications beyond the spiritual is well documented. Such rhetoric, at times, has been used by all sides in a conflict, and is represented on politically orientated sites in Cyber Islamic Environments. It is especially significant in terms of platforms seeking to expand their ideology into other political and social arenas.

## 4.2 Islamic political dimensions online

### 4.2.1 Afghanistan

A good example of 'political Islam' on the Internet would be the various sites associated with the Taliban in Afghanistan. The Taliban has its origins in the complex aftermath of the Soviet occupation of Afghanistan, emerging in 1994 and occupying Kabul in 1996.[1] Seemingly spontaneous in its foundation, and an Islamic phenomenon of the 1990s, some parallels could be drawn between the Taliban and Cyber Islamic Environments. Certainly, several sites have taken it upon themselves to promote this radical Islamist movement. Determining the 'official' credentials of such sites is problematic, but there is no doubt that several maintain links to information sources close to the Taliban's hierarchy, and are regularly updated with (reproductions of) official news bulletins. Taliban Online, produced in Pakistan, claimed over 146,000 hits in a one-year period from its inception in November 1997. The site incorporates extensive details on Taliban policies and Islamic interpretation, notably in the area of *jihād*. News stories in 1998 ranged from defences of Osama bin Laden, accused of the bombing of the US embassies in Kenya and Tanzania, to local news taken from the *Dharb-i-M'umin* service. These stories might not circulate widely outside the region, but provide an insight into Taliban policy:

> Eve-teaser punished: . . . Staff of the Amr-bil-M'aroof Department arrested an Eve-teaser and duly punished him. The culprit was found teasing a woman. With a blackened face he was made to take a round of the market-place saying at the top of his voice, 'O people, never tease any man's mother, sister or wife otherwise you will be punished the same way. I sincerely repent and promise never to even look at any women.' After a thorough beating, the culprit was locked up in jail.[2]

Other aspects of Taliban 'justice' are also located online. News bulletins contained in Taliban Online frequently detail the implementation of *sharī'a* in Afghanistan, including capital punishments. The site acts as a conduit for fund-raising, encouraging donations to an address in Pakistan, advertised as funding medicine and education for the Afghani population, and essential equipment for Taliban military forces:

> 'And do Jihaad with your wealth and your body.' Al-Quraan
>
> 'The man who supplied [necessities of Jihaad] to a Mujahid, certainly he himself did Jihaad.' Al-Hadeeth [*ḥadīth*]
>
> Supply to Taliban, blankets, sleeping bags and army boots[:]

| | |
|---|---|
| Blanket: | |
| Good: | 500.00 |
| Medium: | 250.00 |

Lower: 150.00
Sleeping bag: 620.00
Army boots: 260.00
(Rates are in Pak. Rupees).[3]

Details are provided of various addresses throughout Pakistan, to which aid and financial assistance can be sent.

Ideological pronouncements also have a high profile on the site, including sermons by Hazrat Maulana Mufti Rasheed Aḥmad and Dr Muḥammad Abdul-Wahid Sayyid, which are promoted as having specific 'curative' properties for individuals and society:

> These sermons have wrought an unbelievable change in the lives of countless people.
>
> Innumerable young men adopted the facial characteristics decreed by sunnah.
>
> Many dissolute women who did not observe purdah, started observing it diligently and according to shari'ah.
>
> Thousand of deeply-troubled, lost people found an answers [*sic*] to their problems in these sermons.
>
> In Pakistan and abroad, these sermons have been published in twelve different language [*sic*]. The effective cures mentioned in these valuable sermons are a remedy for the ailments besetting every Muslims of today [*sic*].[4]

Some commentators challenge the extent to which such observance is voluntary in nature. However, the distribution of curative sermons through the net is significant, given the high numbers of hits this site attracts, and the frequent links into the site from other Cyber Islamic Environments. There is no doubt that there is a militaristic angle to this website. The *jihād* section of the site has a green and black 'camouflage' webpage background, and includes over thirty sermons reflecting the Taliban religious perspective on this term (focusing on its militaristic rather than its esoteric dimensions). These include 'A poignant message to the ummah' (a sermon in English and Arabic audio formats) and 'The true meaning of shaheed' (being a martyr, martyrdom), clearly seen as important to promote in cyberspace (and elsewhere) given the Taliban's military campaigns.

Variations in spelling of 'Taliban' provide other websites, some of which may be affiliated with the Taliban. For example, typing *taleban* into a search-engine brings the surfer to the 'Afghan Taleban Online – Taleban Islamic Movement of Afghanistan'. This New York-based site features extensive documentation on every aspect of Taliban policy. Titles include: 'The Islamic state lends full support to the UN agencies and NGOs', 'Restoration of women's safety, dignity and freedom', 'Observance of Islamic hejab or the veil', 'Efforts to combat production and consumption of illicit drugs', and 'The Islamic state is against all forms of terrorism'. The online perspectives of Afghan Taleban Online can present an image of a relatively moderate and accommodating regime, with an Islamic historical continuity going back to the arrival of Islam in the region 1,300 years ago.[5]

Political and military opposition to the Taliban is located online, together with resources reflecting Afghanistan contemporary issues and news. These include Jamiat-e-Islami Afghanistan, presenting a memorial site to '(T)he people who gave their lives up for the cause of Islam and Afghanistan.'[6] To the casual browser, their objectives might be seen as similar to the Taliban:

> Jamiat considers as its duty to provoke the spirit of Jihad in all Afghan brave Muslims in order to assure the progress and strengthening of the world-wide Islamic call, to break the chain of tyranny and oppression, and to wipe out all criminal enemies of Islam. Mujahideen of Jamiat have taken the initiative in this way and have proved their genuineness and sincerity in eradicating the agent band of Khalq, Parcham and the invading Russians.
>
> At the present critical juncture, the country is at the brink of complete destruction. In such a time, Jamiat calls upon the brave youth who are the sincere supporters of Islam; upon the concerned religious scholars who are inheritors of the great Islamic heritage; upon the military officers who are maintainers of our honor and pride; upon educated persons in modern science and technology; upon the honorable farmers and faithful workers; and upon all the noble Afghan nation to gather under the lofty banner of Islam and unite in solid ranks in order to save the country from the present sorrowful state, the continuation of which destroys our history and culture, traditions and sacred values.
>
> We carry on our multi-dimensional struggle with complete confidence in God's help. If we are weak and homeless today,

> tomorrow we will be strong and powerful. This is God's unchangeable law![7]

The alliance of modern science and technology with those working the fields is promoted here, on a platform broadly opposed to the Taliban regime. In Cyber Islamic Environments, different aspects of Afghani Muslim understanding and political perspectives articulate their viewpoints online. Several other opposition groups, not necessarily supportive of each other, can also be located in cyberspace. The Hezb-e Wahdat (Party of Unity) site also provides opposition information, focusing upon a gallery of photos of martyred leader Abdul Ali Mazari (d. 1995). The site proclaims against 'reactionary Shīʿism' and 'these false bearers of peace' (that is, the Taliban), whilst asserting its own complex position within the rubble of the political landscape:

> The Taliban, whose deceitful and murderous face was tainted for the first time with the blood of our people's leader, shall pay a heavy price for their shameful and inexpedint [*sic*] actions and for the death of justice and liberation at the black hearts of the Taliban and their supporters.[8]

As with other geo-political entities, issues associated with cultural and other factors in Afghanistan can be located in cyberspace. Responses to gender issues in Afghanistan have resulted in the creation of several proactive websites, organized by expatriates and sympathizers. The Plight of the Afghan Woman offers numerous links, responding to the treatment of women by the Taliban. Titles include 'Afghanistan's relentless war on women', 'Taleban beat Afghan woman over bare ankles', and 'Women's position, role, and rights in Islam'.[9] Women's issues and Islam online are a significant area for further study. It is important to see that the site's author(s) placed the following caveat on the front page:

> This page is dedicated to the plight of the Afghan Woman. Today, there are more than 40,000 widows in the capital of Afghanistan. Women are forced to cover themselves from head to toe, denied access to education, forbidden to work and support their families, and face brutal beatings if they do not comply with the rules set forth for them by their oppressors. The world needs to know about this tragedy; our

> hope is that this page will become a good source of recent news and information pertaining to the current struggle women in Afghanistan are facing.
>
> PLEASE NOTE: THE CURRENT OPPRESSION OF WOMEN IN AFGHANISTAN IS DUE TO POLITICS AND IGNORANCE, NOT ISLAM!! (their emphasis)[10]

The extent to which this hidden message might be found (or appreciated) by the casual browser is open to question on this powerful site. One link suggests a scapegoat, when discussing practices in the Indian subcontinent:

> One must remember that the ancestors of Indians, Pakistanis and Bangladeshes [*sic*] were Hindus. These people mix bits of Hinduism with Islam and label it Islam. It is time to educate these uninformed Muslims about the true nature of Islam.[11]

The site has a political and social impetus, although it suggests that it does not belong to one particular political grouping. As a statement, aspects of the site such as the 'Photographs of Afghan women' by A. Raffaele Ciriello produce an effective insight (without commentary) on contemporary concerns in the region, and could be effective in mobilizing public opinion outside Afghanistan.[12] The site is extensively hyperlinked by 'academic' linkpages as a resource.

Equally vocal, and containing a wealth of opposition-related information, the Revolutionary Association of the Women of Afghanistan (RAWA) website explicitly focuses against Taliban activities:

> Afghan fundamentalists treat women as degraded souls whose only function is to satiate men's lust and reproduce! Had we been facing some civilized opponents, we might have convinced them of our rights by logic and words of reason. But as fundamentalists go on rampage in Afghanistan, RAWA holds that our women will never be able to achieve their rights through the 'kindness' of the fundamen-talists [*sic*]. To attain a meaningful emancipation, our women must continue their hard, long struggle against fanaticism and carry it to the end. We are at the opinion [*sic*] that any collaboration with the fundamentalists will only lead further ravaging [*sic*] of the Afghans by these bandits.[13]

The site contains material in Persian and English, centring on the 'martyred' leader 'Meena' (d. 1987). Activities including social work and educational projects in refugee camps, both inside and outside Afghanistan, are highlighted, and RAWA statements are well documented. In terms of articulating a position against the Taliban, the site pulls no punches: it includes graphic photographic records of *sharī'a* amputations, and maintains an up-to-date record of its interpretation of Afghanistan-related news.[14]

Many other sites, some presenting an 'official' image, can be found expressing different Afghani perspectives as well as opinions from outsiders. The Taliban cannot be described as a typical governmental source, given the short duration it has been established, not to mention (in terms of the Internet) the various sources representing themselves as Taliban, official and unofficial. Given the paucity of other media sources relating to the region, the Internet represents one arena in which expressions of Muslim identity can be articulated.

### 4.2.2 Pakistan

Pakistan has close historical, social, organizational, cultural and religious ties with Afghanistan. As noted above, some Afghani sites are authored and hosted in Pakistan. Pakistan itself has developed a significant presence in cyberspace, with political organizations identifying the Internet as an area for expansion. Governmental sites contain a broad range of official interpretations of political events, together with religious perspectives and interpretations. Major political parties have placed themselves online, and in addition there are sites organized by those with Pakistani connections outside the country. These present diverse perspectives on Islamic and Muslim issues, often aimed at an international audience.

The Government of Pakistan Official Home Page provides an indication of this Islamic republic's religious orientation and interests, especially through the application of symbols and religious material integrated into the site. The first image encountered is the portrait of Muḥammad 'Alī Jinnāh (1876–1948), who is often described as the founding father of Pakistan. Various calligraphic symbols and 'Names of God' dominate the frames-format, on topics such as 'The fundamentals of religion',

'Islam, the true religion', and 'Islam and life'. According to the pages' author(s), fundamentals include *tawḥīd* (unity), *ṣawm* (fasting during the month of Ramaḍān), *ḥajj* (pilgrimage) and *zakāt* (annual alms).

The site was accessed as part of the research for this book, during the governmental rule of the Muslim League. It is anticipated that future government changes will be reflected in the religious content of official websites such as this. The pages on Ramaḍān link to the Ahl Qur'an wal Sunnah Society (People of the Qur'ān and Sunnā), a 'mirror' from a site based in Detroit, Michigan: detailed interpretations are provided. This suggests that the government site is a reflection of certain other interests, which themselves have close ties with Pakistan. Whilst the government may be, at times, in conflict with Pakistan's Jamā'at-i Islāmī party (JII), it is prepared to link to the writings of JII's founder Mawdūdī, and the related International Institute of Islamic Thought (IIIT) in Virginia (with reproductions of publications relating to jurisprudence).

The Pakistan government's Qur'ān hyperlinks take the surfer to pages discussed elsewhere in this book, such as the Scholarly Technology Group browser, and the Islamic Audio Studio. The site additionally features details of several governmental departments, on the federal government, secretariat, and related policies. Official media links to Ministry of Information departments are provided: these include daily audio files of Radio Pakistan bulletins in Urdu and English, together with news from independent sources such as newspapers. The content of such officially endorsed media includes material on Islam. The government also contributes its own official instructions and regulations relating to *ḥajj* organization. However, the Pakistan government's site focuses upon the Sunnī majority, with little information on the Shī'a population or Christian minorities at the time of writing. Whether this is for political reasons or lack of resources can only be speculated upon.

Specific party lines and interests of the ruling party are incorporated in the webpages: the president of Pakistan, Muḥammad Rafiq Tarar, had one page on the site in 1998, and one speech reproduced. By contrast with Tarar, Prime Minister Muḥammad Nawaz Sharif has an extensive listing, including audio files. Sharif, the 'youthful leader of the Pakistan Muslim

League', was compared in favourable terms to Jinnāh. The Islamic identity of the government is reinforced, but the pages only allude to reasons why Sharif was forced to leave earlier governments. There was an e-mail link to Sharif on the site, so feasibly he could have been asked about this omission (!).[15]

The Pakistan People's Party (PPP), in opposition at the time of writing, describes itself as 'the Voice of the Nation', and has an extensive web presence, produced from Islamabad. The party's position as former governmental party is stressed in the site. The front page shows images of party founder Zulfikar Ali Bhutto (1928–79), who is described as a *shahīd* (martyr), and daughter and leader Benazir Bhutto (1953–). Lengthy biographical data are provided on both father and daughter, including family origins, education, publications and career highlights. The formulation of PPP policy by Zulfikar and relations with Islamic platforms are referred to, together with Zulfikar's socialist ideological concerns. Reference is made to the Council of Islamic Ideology, a PPP creation, and the proclamation of Islam as state religion under Zulfikar.

In the PPP site, biographical information on Benazir includes her home address, telephone, fax and e-mail contact details, suggesting a policy of openness and accessibility, at least in theory. A selection of Benazir's speeches is available on policy concerns, including audio and video files, but very little direct reference to Islam. The archive is updated on a regular basis. Principal banners include 'Human Rights', a PPP Manifesto in eighteen parts, a full listing of regional party leaders, and pages in support of Kashmir's reintegration with Pakistan. Daily news bulletins of PPP-related stories are provided: these express the party's strong opposition to the activities of the Pakistan Muslim League, and discuss aspects of various legal issues surrounding the PPP. The overall impression of the site is its non-Muslim emphasis, in the face of 'political' Islam: for example, there are no references to interpretation of sources, or links to the Qur'ān. References to the integration of cultural and religious minorities are given.[16]

One new figure to emerge into Pakistan politics in the 1990s was the former cricketer Imran Khān, whose party Pakistan Tehreek-e-Insaf (PTI) promotes an Islamic agenda, although there are no statements directly relating to interpretation or quotations from the Qur'ān on the pages. Khān's ethos is demonstrated in the 'Ideology' pages, which state that PTI seeks to

> Support and promote the Islamic way of life according to the principles laid down in the Objectives Resolution . . . Spread a democratic culture by guaranteeing freedom of association and expression. Promote respect for the constitution and laws and provide a credible government which people can trust . . . Promote unity, tolerance, solidarity, and goodwill amongst Pakistani citizens.[17]

Photographs of Imran Khān dominate the pages, and a selection of articles and interview material provided by him are incorporated onto the site. These include his commentary on the PPP (and its perceived 'corruption'), and titles including 'Vision and compromise', 'Selective accountability', and 'The only way to save Pakistan'. Many site pages were 'under construction' at the time of browsing, although notably the page for donations was effective and detailed. As represented in this site, the PTS 'Muslim' political agenda is clearly different from the PPP *and* Muslim League's, demonstrating some of the diversity associated with Islamic political agendas in Pakistan. The entry page to the site includes a substantial quote from Jinnāh and his photograph, implying an association with Imran Khān.

Jamā'at-i Islāmī Pakistan (JII) found it beneficial to set up a site, detailing policy, speeches, history and interpretation of Islam based on Mawdūdī and contemporary Jamā'at leaders.[18] Making strong use of icons and frames, this was one of the first political Muslim sites in Pakistan, and is one of the most pro-active in terms of Muslim political agendas: the site is produced in JII headquarters in Mansoora, a suburb of Lahore. The site is updated on a daily basis, and has a strong Islamic identity, including *Basmallah* ('In the name of God' images). It makes many references to the concept of the *Khalīfa* movements and the Islamic state (as defined by Mawdūdī).

There are declarations in English and Urdu of the JII's aims and objectives, with an overview of its fifty-year history. Much of the site is news-related. Reference is made to the intellectual and spiritual status of women, and there are overtly political statements on the front page, such as 'JII to oust the Nawaz administration'.[19] The JII senator, 'Amir' Khurshid Ahmed, also has a speech audio file on the front page.

Interlinked to these JII introductory pages are the Islam for Children pages (based on explanations about angels, prophets and Muḥammad). Elsewhere, the site presents information relating to decision-making possibilities according to JII agendas. Discussion options are provided in a 'chat-room', where individuals can dialogue on Muslim issues. On the site, questions can be put to the 'Chief' of JII, and an archive of previous questions is available (on religious and other issues). For example, the issue of 'Saying Merry Christmas to Christians' raises the issue of electronic communications:

> Question: While browsing your web pages I was interested to note that the Amir of the Jamaat had wished the Christians a merry Christmas. Personally I see nothing wrong in Muslims being good mannered towards the non-Muslims, and I would tend to agree with the Amir on this point. However, every Xmass [*sic*] we see e-mails being passed around from various Muslim groups that say that Muslims MUST NOT wish anyone a happy non-Islamic festival. While I can challenge their views from a general moral stance I cannot provide them with any specific 'nass' on the subject that would indicate that it is harmless to wish Christians a happy Xmass. Can the Amir provide a justification for this approach that may satisfy a reasonably intelligent Muslim?
>
> Answer: The gesture of being good mannered to the non-Muslims and wishing them a merry Christmas is not meant to exalt their religion. I believe that showing good mannerism to Christian members of human family would help in brushing aside the false and negative Western media propaganda about Islamic organisations which is portraying the Muslims as terrorists, intolerant and extremists in their print and electronic media headlines.
>
> The Muslim community has been raised by the Allah Almighty for the service of humanity. In order to reach to all human community and to preach them true message of Islam, which is a 'deen' of justice and peace, a Muslim must be good mannered to his non-Muslim neighbourhood, fellow counterpart and fellow human beings.[20]

This has particular implications within Pakistan, given the occasionally volatile relations between (elements in) the Muslim and non-Muslim populations. It also acts as an indicator to outsiders relating to the projection of a moderate public-relations image for JII.

Many pages on the JII site relate directly to Islamic interpretations, including pages with reference to women in Islam.

Discussions on marriage, divorce, inheritance and personal law stress the JII view relating to equality as expressed in their interpretation of the Qur'ān. The site emphasizes that Islam (as interpreted by JII) accommodates and promotes the role of women in society.

> In Islam and in a Muslim society, a woman plays the role of a mother, a sister, a wife and a daughter. In the Muslim social setting, a woman is considered woman and guided to progress in that capacity . . . We believe, woman has always been deprived and suppressed in the history. In the past she was subjected to suppression as woman, she was degraded, subjected, enslaved and sexually tortured. But today the apparently charming yet deceptive slogans of the West have deprived her of the feminine identity and character. Every effort is made to convert her to 'he-woman', and all this is done in the name of feminism and basic rights.[21]

The solution to this issue, at least in theory, is located in the JII interpretation of the Qur'ān, as promoted throughout the webpages. This is extended further with the reproduction in Urdu and English of a Charter of Rights:

> The charter declared to end exploitation and improve political representation of women and give them decisive role in the political parties, election and decision-making in the assemblies. Free working in the women wings [*sic*] of political parties would be ensured through necessary legislation.
>
> Women would be provided adequate environment and facilities to protect their rights and undertake social up-lift plans through formation of organizations enabling them to devote full attention within the Islamic confines . . .
>
> The convention regretted that Pakistani women right to veto have been exploited [*sic*] and it has become an established fact that record bogus voting takes place at women polling stations. Jamaat will establish a Women Commission comprising member ladies, who coupled with Islamic orientation and familiar with the needs and problems of the women.[22]

JII's 'female content' was not online at the time of research.

Answers relating to 'mundane' domestic issues are also incorporated in the site. For example, a response to the issue of motorway provision in Pakistan was given, alleging misconduct of

Nawaz Sharif and financial irregularities.[23] Unlike other Pakistani political parties online, the Qur'ān also features on this site, with an English translation of the *Turjuman al-Qur'ān* (commentary on the Qur'ān) – provided in monthly portions to make it 'easier to read'. Under the banner 'Our World View' there are commentaries on the JII position relating to Islam and the West.

The site contains much heavy criticism of the Pakistan administration. The JII Islamic Declaration (*Ijtema*) expresses dissatisfaction with the government's performance, citing corruption and suggesting that there was a loss to national interests. JII states that Pakistan's Muslim League government has 'sold out' because it sought to please American interests. In connection with this activist platform, the site documents supportive activities, including fund-raising, demonstrations and meetings, in video and audio formats.

The JII's recent emphasis on multimedia and the Internet is perhaps indicative of the party's middle-class, educated, English-speaking membership in the Pakistani social élite, and might also be associated with its support networks outside Pakistan where computer access is wider. JII has invested heavily in producing an effective and regularly upgraded and updated site. During a fieldwork visit in 1995, the writer discussed the potential of the 'electronic superhighway' with JII leaders in Mansoora. They had not considered this technology at that time, focusing on other media to propagate their interpretations. For JII, a website is now an effective medium for promoting an interpretation of Islam to a wide audience, and is more cost-effective than other media forms. Cyber Islamic Environments represent economy of *da'wa*.

In an analysis of the Pakistani political milieu, the Muttahida Quami Movement (MQM) has to be considered. The MQM, founded in 1984, is a platform for the aspirations of (a proportion of) the *muhajjir* (migrant) population in Pakistan, and their descendants who arrived in the country as a result of partition. The MQM's particular base is Karachi, which incidentally houses many Pakistani computer companies. The site's focus is on news and responses to the other political parties in the country, emphasizing the human rights abuses that are alleged to have been made by governmental forces against the MQM. Karachi, and Sind province in general, has been the victim of sectarian violence (on both sides) during recent years. The MQM's ideological emphasis on Urdu, resented by other sectors in the population, is stressed in the site, which contains a substantial archive containing Urdu documentation. This is important, given the ethnic-cultural identity concerns this represents.

The MQM site does not comment directly on Islamic matters, but inevitably in the Pakistani context, there is frequently a religious subtext. The MQM's stance on religious issues is claimed to be as follows:

> MQM wants to establish a system in the society whereby all citizens may lead their lives in accordance with their religion, faith and belief. MQM is against exploitation and injustices in the name of religion, faith and sect. It also aims at providing full protection to religious minorities.[24]

The MQM's leader, Altaf Hussain, has been resident in London since 1992. His frequent speeches and documents can now easily be transmitted to Pakistan via the Internet, making it a resource for exiled opposition. Faxes had previously dominated exchanges. Fund-raising is also co-ordinated through the MQM's Khitmat-e-Khalq Committee in London.

'Individualistic' platforms also have a presence in Cyber Islamic Environments related to Pakistan. The Tanzeem-e-Islami site reflects the views of Dr Israr Ahmad, and acts as a channel for his three interrelated organizations: Tanzeem-e-Islami Pakistan, Markazi Anjuman Khuddam ul Quran Lahore, and Tahreek-e-Khilafat Pakistan.[25] The ethos of the organization focuses on the promotion of the Caliphate movement (seeking the return of a supreme religious earthly authority or caliph to rule the Muslim word) and, as such, Israr is against the electoral political system as it now stands in Pakistan. Israr sought the implementation of *sharī'a* law in Pakistan, and what might be interpreted as stricter understandings of the Qur'ān and Sunna, indicating Israr's alienation from JII, of which he was an early member.[26] This is described as 'reflection-through-action', based on Qur'ānic principles.

Israr has taken advantage of the Internet through audio pages which predominantly feature regularly updated sermons and speeches, together with commentaries on aspects of the Qur'ān, in Urdu and English. This includes a speech given at a controversial 'International Khilafah Conference' in Britain in 1994, promoting *jihād*. Locally produced material includes a prayer recited by Israr, and recorded in a mosque, *Dua Salat ul Vitar*, an atmospheric audio file in which emotive responses from other individuals can also be heard.

Clearly, the orientation is centred on Israr's own understanding of Islam, and there are parallels with his other published works. Subjects that reflect these interests include the 'Current Islamic and political situation in Pakistan', 'In favour of the Shariat bill according to Qur'an and Sunnah', and comments on *aḥāḍīth* sources. Using the website, Israr seeks to emphasize his position in relation to contemporary affairs, such as his 'Islamic' perspective on nuclear weapons:

> Dr Israr Ahmad said that the Government should boldly and unequivocally refuse to sign the Comprehensive Test Ban Treaty [CTBT], disregarding all international pressures as well as promises of foreign aid. He said that Pakistan's nuclear capability is a Divine Favor, and signing the CTBT will be in contravention to the Qur'anic imperative of building maximum power.[27]

Clearly, Israr is enthusiastic about the propagation of his particular interpretation of Islam, and applies the website vigorously to reinforce his viewpoints. It reflects his manifesto: 'to remove the existing dichotomy between modern physical and social sciences on the one hand and the knowledge revealed by Almighty Allah (Subḥānahu Wa Ta'āla) on the other.'[28] Given Israr's relatively marginal position in the Islamic spectrum in Pakistan, his application of webpages is logical, but currently diametrically opposed to other Muslim religious leaders in other contexts.

### 4.2.3 Kashmir

In terms of the contemporary situation in Pakistan, the subject of Kashmir is an emotive one, and arguments on both the Indian and Pakistani sides can be found in cyberspace on this sensitive territorial dispute. In Cyber Islamic Environments, this issue is frequently articulated in 'religious' language, applying Islamic terminology, quotes and images. The Jammu Kashmir Liberation Front (JKLF) has a number of sites linked to its interests, focusing on human rights abuses and providing academic and media resources on Kashmiri issues. Two sites share authors based in Bradford, England, although one includes more 'external' material such as links to the UN Peacekeeping Force and Amnesty International, as well as sources located in India.[29] Amidst a copious application of images and colours, the designs includes animated banners 'dripping' blood, photographs of martyrs, and multimedia film from Kashmir's capital Srinagar. There is a feature on Mohammed Maqbool Butt, described as the 'Ho Chi-minh of Kashmir' and the first Kashmiri *shahīd* (martyr). An image of two girls, wearing scarves decorated with Qur'ānic quotations, is on the front page.

Whilst direct references to Islam are limited to a link to the Muslim Students Association (MSA), the JKLF site does have an Islamic identity, in that it makes references to restoring religious rights for all peoples in Kashmir. The site has a rival in the form of an Indian Army Kashmir website, presenting that force's point of view. Hackers infiltrated the site during 1998, and content was altered to present the JKLF perspective.

> Visitors to the altered Website found the homepage dominated by information on alleged torture of Kashmiris by the Indian security forces. The sabotage happened as India and Pakistan began talks in Islamabad to ease tensions . . .
>
> The Indian army launched its Kashmir pages last month to counter allegations of human rights abuses by troops in Kashmir and to give its side of the story. It lists alleged attacks by Kashmiri insurgents and cease-fire violations by Pakistan. But the hackers rededicated the site to 'all the Kashmiri brothers who are suffering the brutal oppression of the Indian army'. Kashmir is at the centre of tensions. And they filled it with statistics on the number of Kashmiris allegedly killed, raped and tortured by Indian troops. The Website's title page featured photographs overwritten with the words 'stop the Indians' and 'save Kashmir'. The pictures showing Kashmiri militants allegedly killed by Indian forces were posted on other pages under headings such as 'massacre', 'torture', 'extra-judicial execution' and 'the agony of crackdown'. Saboteurs also shut down the site's comments book 'due to ill-mannered entries by people who can't face the truth'. The Asian Age newspaper said the website was hacked by an unnamed information service in Lahore, Pakistan. The Indian army temporarily moved to a new address but had restored the original site within hours. A government statement said the hackers changed the site

> parameters so that visitors were diverted to a different server. It said locking systems were being incorporated to prevent any repeat sabotage.[30]

Given the Islamic associations of the Kashmiri dispute, the volatility of the area, its relevance in contemporary Muslim discourse across the web and its application as a rallying point for various political agendas, could it be only a matter of time before other overtly anti-Kashmiri/anti-Muslim sites are hacked? The potential for hacking being a two-way process also exists, forming part of an information war.

### 4.2.4 Malaysia

It is useful to compare and contrast Cyber Islamic Environments relating to Pakistan with those of Malaysia, where computer ownership is wider, and specific research has been undertaken relating to Islamic applications of computer technology. Many organizations have established a presence online, and the technology has been increasingly applied to articulate political arguments in governmental and other circles. This was effectively demonstrated during 1998–9, in the aftermath of the arrest and trial of former Deputy Prime Minister Anwar Ibrahim, instigated by Prime Minister Mahathir Mohamad.[31] This demonstrated the application of governmental websites, the potential of opposition commentaries closely associated with key players, and issues arising out of Islam, censorship and the Internet.

The irony of Mahathir's promotion of information technology (including the Internet), and the negative impact it had on his political agenda, was noted by critics:

> It is true that internet has played a big role in helping to loosen Dr Mahathir's tight grip over the flow of information and ideas in Malaysian society. For someone who wants Malaysia to be at the forefront of the IT revolution, this must be terribly frustrating. There is very little that Mahathir can do to curb or control the transmission of news or analysis through cyberspace.[32]

The website of the Malaysian prime minister's office contains biographical information on Mahathir, cabinet details and governmental links. There is no direct Islamic content, although the speeches do have a Muslim emphasis, whilst accommodating Mahathir's 'Vision 2020' interpretation of multiculturalism. The links to news resources include selected local papers (which did not present a hostile view of Mahathir during the Anwar crisis) and links to international media concerns, such as CNN, Reuters, Time, and Asia Week, all of which carried extensive coverage of all viewpoints in the Anwar crisis. The site is utilized as a vehicle for promoting Mahathir, his life to date and his family. A photograph shows them in western dress, with the backdrop of oil portraits of Mahathir and his wife, around a rug containing Arabic calligraphy from the Qur'ān. Sources relating to the premier include an updated archive of speeches (inaccessible at the time of writing) with a focus on financial issues and western relations. None of the speeches (according to their titles) referred directly to Anwar, who, after the crisis emerged, was quickly edited from the site. The general page does link into another site with references to religion in Malaysia, but the page was blank at the time of research.[33]

The majority of individual Malaysian governmental departments have their own websites, centrally linked. Some of these have a more specific Islamic ethos and motivation than others. For example, when the Department of Islamic Development of Malaysia (JAKIM) launched its own website, it stated that

> It is hoped that this Homepage will be another source of information on Islam which is accurate and noble as a way to counter wrong influences and teachings from the enemies of Islam that can lead to deviation . . .
>
> [Finally] with the launching of this Homepage, the image of Islam will be enhanced and at the same time erase any misconceptions about Islam among the ummah.[34]

The Malaysian government controls several sites relating to Islam and Muslim affairs. Mahathir has a considerable presence on the site, with an archive of speeches, policy documents and information. This includes his comments and analysis of religious matters – rhetoric incorporating 'Islamic language' and concepts. The JAKIM site includes information on *ḥalal* foods, National Mosque sermons, advice on family matters, and an e-mail submission form permitting individuals to send their questions to the JAKIM 'panel of experts', based on *Mazhab Shafie* or the Shāfiʿī 'school of law'.[35]

Lists of 'deviationist teachings' also feature on the site. This is a controversial area, given the different emphases on political Islam in Malaysia. The teachings are defined as follows:

> Deviationist teachings refers to any teachings or practices which are propagated by Muslim or non-Muslims who claim that their teachings and practices are Islamic or based on Islamic teachings, whereas in actual fact the teachings and practices which they propagate are contrary to Islam which is based on the Al-Quran and al-Sunnah and against the teachings of Ahli Sunnah Wal Jamaah.[36]

This presents a non-inclusive viewpoint, indicative of 'official' Islam in Malaysia, and reacting strongly against elements that in other contexts are important in Islam and Muslim world views. The 'deviationist teachings' pages reflect governmental concerns relating to Ṣūfi-orientated interpretations of Islam. These have been associated with banned organizations, including Darul Arqam, whose members were forced to undergo detention and 're-training' in Islamic orthodoxy. The pages place the blame for deviation on 'syncretism', 'Hindu-Buddha', 'animism and dynamism' (*sic*), which is somewhat ironic, given the multicultural (multi-religious) nature of Malaysian society promoted by the government elsewhere. 'It [deviation] emerges through the practices of black magic and the traditional art of self-defence.'[37] Locating such 'deviationist teachings' online is difficult, at least in Malaysian Cyber Islamic Environments. Whilst Darul Arqam have been described as technological Ṣūfis, their presence on the Internet is severely restricted because of governmental controls.[38]

The Malaysian government's official opinions on Islam are also represented by the IKIM (Institut Kefahaman Islam Malaysia) site, which presents speeches by Mahathir, including video stream material in English and Bahasa Malay.[39] Topics of a specifically Islamic nature are contained here, including 'The administration of Islamic law', 'Towards the twenty-first century', 'Islamic world and global co-operation', and 'Tolerance though understanding'. These links were all 'broken' at the time of writing, although whether this was through technical inputting error or through manipulation of site material was difficult to ascertain. The United Malays National Organization, Mahathir's political party, also had several websites at local and national levels, which largely reflected the official Barisan Nasional (National Coalition) policy.[40]

In opposition, the primary Muslim political party is Parti Islam SeMalaysia (PAS), who promote their activities on a variety of sites at central and local levels. PAS controls the local government in the state of Kelantan, but PAS material is additionally produced from contributors in other Malaysian states, where it is in a political minority. It includes more sermons, reflecting the demands of this *sharīʿa*-orientated group, who pronounce, in opposition, that they are the 'real' Muslim party in Malaysia. Not having to be so concerned about coalitions with non-Muslim parties from the diverse cultural, religious and/or ethnic dimensions represented in the country, PAS ideology focuses on a specific Islamic agenda, reflected in their websites containing material in Malay and English. At a national level, these include organizational information, advice on religious matters, details of activities, and parliamentary links.[41] At a local level, information includes photos of activities, including gatherings and 'festivals', together with co-ordinating data relating specifically to local events.[42]

The 'Anwar effect' during 1998–9 led to the mobilization of opposition through the Reformasi (reform) platform. Details of Anwar's imprisonment, updated daily, were included on a variety of sites, some presenting a more overtly Muslim nature than others. Websites can permit activism where other media forms are suppressed. Given that e-mail is also a significant form of communication for Malay Muslim students, networking both inside and outside Malaysia, developments in Malaysia have provided an early model for surveying the political impact of Internet technology in a computer-literate society. All dimensions of the Anwar situation have been reported, in governmental sites, official media, 'independent' media and opposition frameworks.

Anwar himself emerged from the activist organization ABIM (Angkatan Belia Islam Malaysia, or the Muslim Youth Movement of Malaysia). ABIM incorporates a particular 'reform' approach to Islamic interpretation, including advocacy of independent legal decision-making or *ijtihād*, based on interpretation of Islamic primary sources.[43] This is demonstrated in Anwar's book *The Asian Renaissance*, which was published online during the crisis. The print publication was one alleged cause for his imprisonment. The book applies strong Islamic imagery and language, and makes heavy implicit criticism of Mahathir's policies:

> The pursuit of economic prosperity is no justification for the persistent and flagrant deprivation of political and civil liberties. In fact, increasing wealth should be the occasion for the extension of freedoms to all spheres, these being the legitimate expectations of a civil society. Notwithstanding the moral basis envisaged in our concept of civil society, these include the expectations that certain fundamental liberties and rights are inviolable and cannot be taken away without due process of law. The Prophet of Islam in his Hajja al-Wida (Farewell Pilgrimage) said: 'O Mankind, your blood, your property and your honour are as sacred as this Holy Land.'[44]

Written prior to Anwar's incarceration, the terminology acquired a new potency when he was imprisoned, and this is highlighted on several sites. A plethora of other sites relating to Anwar Ibrahim emerged during the crisis, from both Malaysian and non-Malaysian perspectives. These included news resources, discussion groups (utilizing e-mail) and statements from a variety of interested parties. One news site, which claimed 320,000 hits in a six-week period, indicated that the site was necessary to realign what were seen as distorted or restrained official sources on Anwar:

> To address this imbalance of reporting by the Malaysian mass media, we have created this web-site to keep all concerned people informed on what the non-Malaysian newspapers and magazines in the world have been publishing on the 'saga' of Anwar Ibrahim.
>
> This web-site has been created by a number of individuals who wish Anwar and the people of Malaysia well. It is not created or sponsored by Anwar, or by any group of persons living in Malaysia.[45]

This raises issues not just surrounding Anwar Ibrahim, but also connected with wider concerns of censorship, media access and perceptions of Malaysian identity. The Gerak platform, a broad coalition of political interests crossing cultural and religious differences, sought to boycott Malaysian newspapers. Many sites presented transcripts and recordings of Anwar's trial and reactions to it.[46] At least forty 'Anwar' sites emerged, compiling interviews, articles and speeches (official and unofficial), some of them linked to Reformasi platforms.[47] These were updated regularly, and photos of demonstrations rapidly had a web presence.[48] Anwar's immediate family had direct control of their own webspace, authored by one of Anwar's daughters. Activism through the web included a site providing Reformasi 'electronic postcards', which could be forwarded by the browser to another e-mail address.[49]

ABIM was closely associated with Anwar Ibrahim, an active member until he joined the United Malays National Organization (UMNO), which was part of the ruling Barisan National governmental coalition. This activist platform is a national network operating both within and outside Malaysia: its website provides links and commentary on the Anwar issue, and also acts as a medium for other information on Islam-related issues, containing commentaries illustrating ABIM's version of 'Islamic reform'. This includes the publication online of three journals – *Berita Malaysia* and *Risala* in Bahasa Malay, and *Islamic Review* in English. Broader issues included 'Muslim world news', a review of global Muslim issues from an ABIM perspective.[50]

Given the broad range of material that features in Cyber Islamic Environments in Malaysia, it is certainly an area that should be monitored closely in terms of computer-mediated communication. Many important Malaysian organizations are wired, allowing for the rapid dissemination of information about contemporary issues associated with Muslims and Muslim organizations in the region.

### 4.2.5 Singapore

The diverse Cyber Islamic Environments associated with Malaysia have been shaped by the Malaysian Federation's proximity, historically, culturally and geographically, to Singapore, which has a Muslim minority population primarily of Malay origin. Given Singapore's long-standing governmental commitment to information technology, it provided an example of one of the earliest Muslim governmental agencies to go online: Majlis Ugama Islam Singapura (Islamic Religious Council of Singapore or MUIS) was one of the forerunners, in terms of its provision of information relating to Islam. MUIS provides information about mosques, family development, opening times for individuals to obtain advice from mosque officers, and information about mosque schools (*madāris*). MUIS was one of the earliest sites to place official sermons online: content is in English and Malay.[51] The site also has a *fatāwā* search-engine database, through which surfers could seek the opinions of the republic's official religious leader (or *Muftī*).

The MUIS official site is in marked contrast to the few alternative Muslim perspectives available online in Singapore, and indicates the strict controls in the non-Muslim-majority republic – where, particularly in the case of Islam, certain divergent viewpoints have been suppressed. Here is a state systemization of religion, where all channels are mediated and controlled through the non-Muslim government. There is an implicit recognition that the needs of the Muslim communities in Singapore have to be officially addressed online like other religious interests, and this is further endorsed by the government-appointed hierarchy, headed by the *Muftī*. The Internet offers a further channel of communication between leadership and grass-roots, particularly in the field of decision-making options.

### 4.2.6 Sudan

The endorsement of the Internet by an official religious hierarchy in Singapore is in marked contrast to other contexts – where it has been seen as a threat to traditional values and interpretations of Islam. As has been seen above, levels of access to the Internet vary considerably in different Muslim contexts, not just because of economic factors, but because of social control. This is particularly evident in the Islamic Republic of Sudan, one arena for dialogue on the Internet's validity in Muslim contexts. Governmental and other pressures have restricted the wealthier levels within Sudanese society who have the income and inclination to go online. During 1998, Sudan obtained its own Internet server, which further mobilized opposition to the web. Mohamed Salih Ḥassan, described as the *imām* of the Ansār sect in Sudan, was concerned that the Internet would unduly westernize and influence Sudanese youth, and instigated a campaign amongst his peers to ban the technology: 'The Muslim people should respect the faith, and not allow such information to reach their families', he said. 'If an uncontrollable system like Internet is introduced in society . . . it will be very difficult for us to preach the Kingdom of Allah.'[52]

An Internet user, 'Sadiq' (not his real name), was interviewed in Sudan:

> We are not calling on those who are afraid of Internet to join. Let them stay away . . . We are all Muslims and I see no reason for things to be imposed on us.
>
> . . . He [the interviewee] is one of many professionals . . . who have had to forego using the Internet at home (many Sudanese adults live with their parents) due to parental opposition. 'My father has warned me from using the Internet. He has threatened to beat me,' the 37-year old told IPS.[53]

According to the report, Sadiq took his computer to a friend's house, to explore the web and avoid parental restriction. This example highlights important issues relating to access, and the restraints within different political and cultural Islamic contexts. Issues emerge relating to intergenerational differences of understanding, together with wider societal pressures and family pressures relating to Sadiq's Internet access. Clearly, from a political angle, the enthusiasm in some sections of Muslim societies for the Internet is not universal.

### 4.2.7 Saudi Arabia

Saudi Arabia is another arena in which these arguments are played out. Patterns of Internet access are slowly changing, and during 1998 Saudi Arabia opened invitations to tender for national Internet providers. The commercial aspects of such provision have long been recognized by Saudi companies, who seek to build on the opportunities technological innovation provides in a global marketplace. Interest in the potential of the Internet was articulated from within the immediate Saudi royal family. Kingdom Holdings, owned by Prince Alwaleed bin Talal (King Fahd's nephew), invested heavily in the Netscape Communications Corporation and Apple Computers. In 1998, he was active with Netscape's decision to join up with the America Online service provider and Sun Computers in order to create a serious competitor to Microsoft. Prince Alwaleed has also been keen to promote regional satellite communications, which could be utilized for the Internet, through the SilkiNet holding company.

Some might see a paradox in Prince Alwaleed's interests, and the restraint that Saudi Arabian society has exercised in terms of allowing their subjects access to the Internet. On the other hand, regionally this could mean that the control of aspects within Internet service provision will become part of the Saudi royal sphere of interest, extending outside the geographical borders of Saudi Arabia. The restraints have emerged primarily from the zone of religious authority, which has hesitated to introduce easy access to the web for Saudi subjects.

> Saudi Arabia has now completed a study on how to prevent objectionable material that is against the country's religious and moral values from entering the kingdom through the Internet.
>
> Efforts are ongoing to provide the best of modern technology, while ensuring that this does not conflict with the traditions and culture of the region . . .[54]

Singapore was seen as a model for ensuring that 'appropriate access' to the web was guaranteed. In 1999, the options in terms of religious material emerging directly from Saudi sources were limited. There is a need in any analysis to distinguish between expatriate-authored sites, and those produced by organizations located within Saudi Arabia. There are a number of grey areas here, for example the sites produced by Saudi Arabian embassies. A number of portals to Saudi information on Middle Eastern services, such as Arabia Online, provide material generated from academic and news sources with strong Saudi connections. Few of these are located inside Saudi Arabia, and do not present opposition perspectives (those against the current regime) which additionally maintain a strong web presence.

Up until 1999, inhabitants in Saudi Arabia who wished to surf the Internet had to access Internet service providers outside the kingdom. This was potentially an expensive process, involving long-distance telephone calls. However, several local Internet service providers emerged, supervised by the King Abdul-Aziz City for Science and Technology. A projected twenty service providers were licensed to come online in Saudi Arabia during 1999.[55]

In terms of Cyber Islamic Environments, examples of websites in Saudi Arabia include the King Faisal Institute, a multi-million-dollar organization which has a remit to 'preserve Islamic culture' through the funding of various philanthropic projects. The site's interface is dominated by a photograph of King Faisal ibn Abd Al Aziz (1906–75) praying; his son, King Fahed ibn Abd Al-Aziz Al Saud, appears on initial entry to the site, together with *basmallah* Arabic calligraphy. The site includes images from the Qur'ān, and uses the English language throughout.[56]

The impact of the current developments in Internet service provision on Cyber Islamic Environments, especially the generation of further Sunnī 'authorities' online, is another area which will require observation and analysis in the coming years. The prospect of minority and dissident voices emerging from within the kingdom onto the Internet is also significant.

## 4.3 'Dissident' voices

In relation to Saudi Arabia and Islam online, the greater proportional presence in cyberspace is that of opposition to elements of the current ruling family and government. Muhammad Al-Mass'ari of the CDLR (Campaign for Democracy and Legal Rights) made extensive use of e-mail and faxes to propagate his views against the Saudi regime (and others). Based in London, Mass'ari's activities have been restricted because of financial insolvency, but up until 1997 he was regularly publishing *Monitor* online. This review and commentary on aspects of Saudi politics was vociferous enough for Mass'ari and his organization to be targeted by the British government, anxious not to alienate Britain's diplomatic and economic relations with Saudi Arabia. Mass'ari also made other pronouncements interpreted as overtly hostile to the UK, and his name was linked with other 'Islamic organizations' and 'terrorist' agendas. The CDLR site is hosted by Islamic Gateway, and contains material to download and browse in various formats in Arabic and English. Its central message is aimed directly at the Al Sa'ūd family. The CDLR accused them of the following:

> Invited the infidel American forces to occupy the holy land of Al-Haramain!
>
> Abuse the visitors of the holy precincts in Makkah and Madinah and treat them with utmost contempt!
>
> Insult and reject Muslims, while respecting and co-operating with the Kuffar [unbelievers]!
>
> Betrayed the trust of the Ummah by steeling over five hundred Billions Dollars from its wealth!
>
> Watched, inactive, the burning and trampling to death of thousands of Hujjaj in the recent Mina fire 1997!
>
> . . . and many, many more crimes! [*sic*][57]

CDLR might qualify as a Cyber Islamic Environment in its assertion of basing activities (and ideals) firmly on the Qur'ān and Sunna. According to CDLR, it seeks to promote 'Islamic human rights' in Saudi Arabia, and 'abides by the method of peaceful and constructive criticism and dissociates itself from all and any attempt to effect reform by force'.[58] In undertaking this agenda, CDLR promotes the application of varied mass media but has been banned from publishing or broadcasting within Saudi Arabia. This makes the application of the Internet very important (although not the only means of communication).

A split within CDLR led to the formation of the Movement for Islamic Reform in Arabia (MIRA), which has similar objectives and indeed a very similar website format, although it appears to have better resources. MIRA contains further articles and updates, such as 'Prince of the month', highlighting alleged corrupt Sa'ūd family members. The site provides a 'History of dissent in Saudi Arabia' [*sic*], and material clearly sympathetic with the objectives of Osama bin Laden, a Saudi Arabian expatriate blamed for attacks on United States embassies during 1998.[59] For some surfers, there may be conflict of interest in reading sites such as MIRA, advocating human rights on the one hand, and supporting the position of Osama bin Laden on the other. MIRA also seeks to analyse current events with a weekly, updated 'Arabia in the media' section, including commentary on religious matters.

CDLR and MIRA can be examined in conjunction with the Al-Saūd House website, organized by the Committee against Corruption in Saudi Arabia. (CACSA). This site focuses on the web as a means of disseminating regularly updated materials, from a broad range of sources, many of which refer to 'Islamic' ideals and concepts, although in different language from the Saudi Arabian 'official' sites:

> C.A.C.S.A. is a peaceful organization whose sole purpose is to change the Saudi Arabian status quo using the Internet as a worldwide campaign tool. C.A.C.S.A. is not associated or affiliated with any political or religious group. C.A.C.S.A. condemns violence, fundamentalism, and extremism and supports the interests of both the United States and Saudi Arabia.[60]

CACSA proactively applies e-mail to lobby political and media sources, listing avenues and addresses which surfers might apply to disseminate their opinions (including ambassadors). The topic of corruption figures strongly in this site, focusing on the ruling family in Saudi Arabia, and producing a 'scale of corruption' of individuals based on a set of criteria. Important central Saudi family figures are alleged by CACSA to have been involved in nebulous and corrupt activities, and the site also lists alleged 'front men', in industry and merchant families, who aid in these alleged affairs.[61]

One example is the entry for 'Abd al 'Azīz ibn Sa'ūd, which alleges that he falsified records suggesting he was a direct descendant of the Prophet Muḥammad:

> To hide his inconsequential background, Abdul Aziz resorted to falsifying records. This kind of corrupt behavior is too evident today in almost all of his children and especially the Sudeiri Seven. Having failed to convince the world of this unconscionable act, the al-Saud today ignore totally the subject except when they are reminded that the Hashemites are the true Guardians of Mecca and Medina.[62]

The site's authors accuse other individuals of profiting from prostitution, drugs smuggling and kickbacks from arms-deals. Many 'scandals' are extensively documented in the site's archives. In the area of human rights, the position of dissidents is discussed, victims of alleged torture are listed, and questions relating to abducted children are introduced (through related links).

Whilst these are all important areas in terms of their religious implications, Islamic religious concerns are also addressed directly, notably a copy of a Religious Petition signed by the Saudi Arabian Muftis (including Sheikh Abdul Aziz ibn Baz), which contained twelve articles promoting Islamic concepts. Issues addressed include corruption, aspects of media control, human rights, foreign policy and justice, which the petition's signatories wanted improved according to an 'Islamic Shar'īa' model. This petition has been taken onto the site by CACSA, and could be interpreted, in view of other materials on the site, as an implicit critique of the Saudi regime by the signatories.

The issue of Islam and politics within governmental settings could be expanded, to analyse all nations with Muslim populations. Many other contexts have similar concerns to some of those discussed above, and models of Internet activism and

Muslim websites could be constructed.[63] At this point in the discussion, it is proposed to examine briefly some of the diverse Muslim platforms operating online outside immediate governmental or opposition contexts, including those that can be defined as paramilitary concerns. Unlike the activism and expression of CACSA, certain sites and organizations possess a military agenda and an Islamic agenda, and they create their own specific Cyber Islamic Environments. They are often linked into more conventional Cyber Islamic Environments, including student pages.

Issues associated with Palestine and Israel maintain an extensive web presence. Given the Palestinian and Jewish Diaspora, the web would seem a perfect medium for rapid dissemination of information – and would also engender communal senses of identity.[64] Many Palestinian organizations with Muslim associated agendas have recognized this, and a variety of opinions can be located online. Outside the political and academic sites associated with the Palestinian government, there are several websites with Muslim identities directly associated with political and paramilitary activities.

Hamas has a number of sites associated with it, with varying degrees of official capacity. For example, the Unofficial Hamas Website (closely linked to the official site in Arabic) provides the following mission statement:[65]

> This website is not affiliated to any national government. Its sole purpose is to provide information and educate the general public on the nature of the organization and bring light to the fact the Palestinian people are living in horrific conditions under Israeli occupation. The site providers do not and will not accept any financial support from any government and rely solely on contributions from private individuals concerned about bringing the truth to the public . . .
>
> The developers of this web site are not affiliated with Hamas in any way. They are a group of individuals concerned about bringing the truth to the public. They do not and will not accept any funding from any source, especially from governments or individuals representing any governments. The goal is to educate the public and provide a more equitable point of view to the situation in the Palestine.[66]

Despite these assertions, the material contained on the site closely reflects Hamas ideologies. The pages open with *basmala* calligraphy, and a photograph of the Al-Aqṣā Mosque in Jerusalem. Subjects include 'The birth of the Zionist entity in Palestine', 'Facts about Israel', 'Test your knowledge of the Middle East', 'Palestinian news', and 'Images from the uprising'. The message is effective, in that each short paragraph presents its point succinctly, so that the casual browser is not overwhelmed with too much information (a criticism that could be levelled elsewhere on the web!). Whilst it is assumed that this site is produced outside Palestine, and the pages state that it is not affiliated with any platforms, the very short paragraphs contained in each linking headline demonstrate an editorial standpoint sympathetic with Hamas. There is, however, no direct 'Islam' content, such as Qur'ān links or quotations. So can it be described as a Cyber Islamic Environment? The Hamas acronym stands for Harakat al-Muqawama al-Islami or Islamic Resistance Movement, and the Arabic word has connotations associated with bravery or courage. There is a paradox operating here of an 'Islamic' organization represented, albeit unofficially, by a site without immediate religious content or indications of affiliation. The site does link to Islam-related Palestinian sites, and the link to the official Hamas pages provides access to Arabic documentation with an overtly Muslim nature.[67] This includes references to the Masjid Al-Quds (Mosque of Al-Quds) in Jerusalem, and a plethora of uploads of speeches and articles with activist titles. A linked *Palestine Today* page contains extensive daily news, suggesting that this 'official Hamas site' is well resourced and produced.

The Islamic Association for Palestine, produced by expatriates in Texas, also contains news in Arabic, pictures and patriotic songs; sound files include the journalist Robert Fisk commenting on Lebanon, Yasser Arafat's comments on Hamas, and a sound recording (from Israeli Broadcasting) of Hamas leader Sheikh Yassin. This site presents a more overtly religious perspective, including detailed opinions on Jerusalem's position within Islam, based upon interpretation of the Qur'ān, focusing on the Al-Aqṣā mosque. A banner proclaiming 'The Islamic Cause' dominates the site's opening page, adjacent to the *basmala* and photos of Jerusalem. The site offers hyperlinks to several journals, including the *Assabeel* magazine, which broadly reflects Hamas opinion.[68]

There are a number of formatting parallels between the Hamas unofficial website and the Hezbollah's 'unofficial' website, suggesting a shared authorship. There is very little in the way of Islamic content, and the site also includes a disclaimer:

> The developers of this web site are not affiliated with Hezbollah in any way. They are a group of individuals concerned about bringing the truth to the public. They do not and will not accept any funding from any source, especially from governments or individuals representing any governments. The goal is to give a more equitable point of view to the situation in the Southern Lebanon.[69]

The site details Hezbollah (Ḥizb Allāh or Party of God) aims and activities in Lebanon, and links into the official Arabic version, which, unlike Hamas, *does* have an English-language version.

The official Hizbollah Central Press Office utilizes Qur'ānic calligraphy (adjacent to a logo in the shape of a machine-gun, spelling out *Ḥizb Allāh* in Arabic), and defines itself strongly as 'an Islamic freedom fighting movement founded due to the Israeli military seizure of Lebanon in 1982 . . .'[70] Another dimension within this site was within the field of Christian–Muslim relations, with the reproduction of a letter from Ḥizb Allāh to Pope John Paul II discussing commonalties and making an attempt at dialogue, in the light of a papal visit to Lebanon. The official site contains a 'resistance statement' (in Arabic), and photographs of the Qana massacre of 1996, in which 106 people were killed in an Israeli attack: the photos include dead bodies, damaged houses and books (including a Qur'ān) within the smouldering ruins.[71] These clearly would produce an emotive reaction, especially amongst many Muslim surfers. An extra dimension for some would be the association of this attack with concepts of martyrdom.

This association with martyrdom is strongly articulated in related Ḥizb Allāh sites. The Islamic Resistance Support Association site incorporates details of its activities in Arabic and English, and is updated daily to provide Ḥizb Allāh perspectives on Lebanese issues. These include transcripts of reports from foreign media. One particular feature of this site is its messages directed at those individuals sympathetic to Israeli aims, in particular people living in Israel. Particular reference is made to an Israeli marine raid into Lebanon at Insariye, which was thwarted by Ḥizb Allāh in 1998. Twelve commandos, members of an élite marine squad, were killed. Extensive details of what went wrong for the Israelis are provided, together with the Islamic justification for the success of the Ḥizb Allāh:

> Salutation to the five martyrs of Kfour, few weeks ago, to the brave and honest Mujahideen who were positioned at every suspected place of infiltration, and to the great martyrs of Occupied Jerusalem, who executed their operation a day before which made the enemy feel that he is on the path of defeats [*sic*].[72]

Photographs of the remains of the commandos are shown on this website, with the caption 'Soldiers' families':

> Be aware that you are dispatching your beloved sons to their destined final place. The death is awaiting them behind every rock, at every valley and mountain and at every inch of our soil their foots stepped on. The land is ours . . . So, get out . . .[73]

This demonstrates effective application of propaganda material, and awareness that many Israeli surfers, including military personnel, will visit the site. The webmaster describes the 'humanitarian' reasons behind the depiction of these photos online:

> These photos show every part alone, just to be sure that the 'Israeli' Army not only doesn't respect your beloved sons when they are alive but when they are dead as well. Obviously, it sends disdainfully and recklessly your beloved sons to the death.
>
> Moreover, the commanders don't even venerate their soldiers when they pass away for the military command had covered up the truth and didn't inform you that your buried sons' corpses had mixed with others or not completed.[74]

Desecration of bodies, mutilation and improper burial are issues both within Judaism and Islam, but the depiction is seen as appropriate on the Ḥizb Allāh site. This emotive material would clearly impact upon Israeli surfers.

The Islamic Resistance Support Association site also features one of several galleries of Muslim 'martyrs' on the web, with an A–Z index of their names and photos. Extensive biographical information on the individual martyrs is provided, together with their places of death, and their marital status. The photos are placed within a symbolic artwork frame, representing a shroud and doves.[75] 'Martyrdom' also features in other sites, including the Hamas-centred Al Kassam Shuhada Memorial: '. . . the only site in the web devoted to the brave mujhidun who fought and gave their life, during the Holy War for our land . . . Allahu Akbar.'[76]

This site makes extensive use of Islamic iconography, such as pages from the Qur'ān, and calligraphy, together with a 'burning memorial flame'. Each fighter in the gallery is described as a *shahīd*. One of the 'martyrs' depicted is Yahya Abd al-Latif Sati Ayyash (1966–96), known as the 'Engineer' because of his abilities with explosives; he was responsible for many car bombs, and was eventually assassinated by Israeli forces in Gaza. The site is run by the Al-Kassam Brigade (Kataib al-Kassam), a militaristic wing associated with Hamas. It clearly explains its definition of *jihād* as being *jihād bil-sayf* or '*jihād* with the sword', although recognizing other forms of the concept:

> We the followers of the great shahid Izz Al-Din Al-Kassam, chose the 'JIHAD WITH THE SWORD', which we thought was the only effective way. The way that is inspired by the history of Islam and Allah's commandments in the KORAN. The way of hard, bloody war – the JIHAD.[77]

This assertive statement of what some commentators describe as militant Islam demonstrates that the spectrum of Cyber Islamic Environments is broad and encompassing, even though not all other shades of opinion would necessarily endorse the viewpoints of the Al-Kassam Brigade.

Similar issues do emerge in other contexts, and it is impossible to survey them all here. However, a couple of areas worthy of reference in terms of this forms of Islamic interpretation include sites associated with El-Djama'a El-Islamia El Mosalaha or Groupe Islamique Armée (GIA). This Algerian organization is one consequence of the cancellation of democratic elections in the country, and the control of power by a government associated with the Algerian military. The GIA policy has been centred on violent tactics against government and other targets, fulfilling a *fatwā* issued by the group's founder Shaykh Abdel Haq el-Ayadia. At the time of research, it appeared that GIA-related sites were inaccessible, suggesting one example of censorship online. An (allegedly) related American Islamic Group (AIG) was also 'closed' at the time of research. It is feasible that the GIA could locate a friendly server over time, in order to promote their message globally, so this absence might be a temporary one.[78] However, the Front Islamique du Salut political party that won the election in 1992 does have a substantial web presence explaining its policies and linking into friendly media. The photographs of victims of the crisis are extremely graphic. The Islamic content of the site, in terms of Qur'ānic quotations, images and sermons, is limited to the provision of a quotation from the Qur'ān.[79] There are a number of other sites in cyberspace devoted to Algerian issues, especially in the French language.

Islam has formed a significant component in discourses and conflicts elsewhere, and the breadth of related websites demonstrates this. Together with the Algerian crisis, the break-up of Yugoslavia (and its aftermath) was an early example of the power of computer-linked communications to spread news rapidly to interested parties. Organizations such as Bosnia-Net utilized e-mail in order to propagate their perspective, bombarding (and in many cases overloading) servers.[80] Related Muslim organizations also used these facilities – although it is not in any way suggested that religion forms a significant part of every platform associated with the crisis. The Internet forms part of contemporary dialogues relating to Bosnia, including the expatriate population.[81] A Bosnian Webring links related sites together.[82] During the Sarajevo siege, e-mail was used to inform outsiders of the situation. The extent to which Islam informs the identity of individual websites varies considerably, with some promoting the concept of a multi-religious society, and others seeking a stronger Muslim identity, or even a 'Bosnian Jihad'.

Platforms that seek to transcend ethnic or national boundaries also exert a presence on the Internet, and apply it to inform their own members, and recruit newcomers in different political and social contexts. Certain platforms network with diverse political perspectives elsewhere, including minority contexts. Thus, the London-based Al-Khilafah Movement in the United Kingdom, seeking a return to the ideals of a single Muslim leader or caliph, provides a regularly updated website, primarily a medium for distribution or perusal of its magazine, but also containing daily news updates. The movement is associated with Ḥizb ut-Ṭahrīr (Party of Purity), which has established a presence amongst Islamic societies on UK campuses. The organization's proclamations in support of various 'jihāds', and its assertion of militant Islamic positions in Bosnia, Israel-Palestine, Kashmir and Afghanistan has led to severe criticism by opponents, including other Muslim groups as well as Jewish student groups. Ḥizb ut-Ṭahrīr has also attacked elements in various Muslim platforms in the UK, especially what they perceive as ineffective leadership. The Ḥizb ut-Ṭahrīr website clearly states its agenda and history:

> Hizb ut-Tahrir is a political party, with Islam as its ideology, whose aim is to resume the Islamic way of life and to convey Islamic da'wah to the world. It works within the Islamic Ummah and together with her, so that she adopts Islam as her cause and is led to restore the Khilafah and the ruling by what Allah (swt) revealed. The Islamic Thought is the soul of its body, its core and the secret of its life.[83]

Ḥizb ut-Ṭahrīr was banned in Jordan, where it was founded by Sheikh Muhammad Taqiuddin (1909–77) in 1953. The presence on the web (and other activities) of Ḥizb ut-Ṭahrīr have alarmed many Muslim-majority countries that have friendly diplomatic relations with the United Kingdom. Ḥizb ut-Ṭahrīr was accused of making anti-Semitic statements, to the alarm of Jews both within and outside the United Kingdom.

A more extreme interpretation of the *Khilafah* ideology is expressed by the breakaway organization Al-Muhājiroun led by 'Sheikh' Omar Bakri Muhammad.[84] Its objectives include:

> Bonding the Muslim community in the west with the Muslims globally in order to create an unbeatable bond within the Ummah and for them to be part of the preparations for the world-wide Islamic revolution.
>
> This can be achieved by addressing the vital issues effecting [*sic*] Muslims world-wide such as that of the conspiracies of their corrupted regimes and rulers, the occupation of their land by the non-Muslims and by the arrangement of funds and help for the world-wide Islamic movements in their struggle against these corrupted rulers and occupiers.[85]

Al-Muhājiroun's website illustrates the organization's objectives, and makes copious references to the Qur'ān. The site is networked to the Islamic Gateway (through provision of web-space), and is regularly updated with interpretations of current events. Subjects in 1999 include support for Osama bin Laden, the 'persecution' of Al-Muhājiroun members by various authorities and alleged bribes being offered by America for information on terrorist activities. Back issues of a related magazine, *As Sahwa*, included potentially controversial topics that might be difficult to express in other media. Titles included: 'Muslims will hound Blair wherever he goes!' and 'British Government's New laws to stop Islamic Activity!' There was also an article about the Conference of Islamic Revivalist Movements attended by the Omar Bakri Muḥammad, Abu Hamza of the Supporters of Shariah, and representatives of the CDLR and the Taliban.[86]

Omar Bakri Muḥammad also acts as self-styled judge of the 'Shari'ah Court of Britain', a registered charity operating with 'The Society of Muslim Lawyers'. He claims the power to issue a 'juristic fatwa' (which he describes as a 'Divine Decree') and provides the 'evidence' justifying assassination of the *Satanic Verses* author Salman Rushdie.[87] Omar Bakri Muḥammad's son also established a website associated with his father's activities. Much of this was under construction at the time of writing, but material included links to related organizations, biographical details on Omar Bakri Muḥammad, and 'Islamic Concepts' on a variety of issues.[88]

## 4.4 Concluding comments

Despite the difficulties in defining politics in certain religious contexts in contemporary understandings of the term, the Internet is clearly important in disseminating a broad range of Islamic political-religious opinions and concerns to a global audience. The above brief survey has shown that many politically active Muslim organizations now regard the web as an integral part of their information strategies. The Internet's application, in conjunction with related computer applications such as 'chat rooms' and e-mail, makes a significant impact in creating a cohesive electronic identity in cyberspace for Islamic political agendas and concerns. Whether this means that it also contributes to a global electronic *umma* could be open to question: many political platforms *are* interlinked, but the concept of a free-flowing dialogue and shared agendas between all shades of opinion remains an aspiration rather than a reality. Whilst issues regarding accessibility still remain, increasingly for participants as well as observers with access to the Internet, Cyber Islamic Environments are a primary medium for religious, political and ideological guidance.

# 5

# *Digital* minbar*: Islamic obligations and authority online*

## 5.1 Projecting authority

A *minbar* is the mosque equivalent of a pulpit, often complex in its wooden construction, from which an imām delivers a Friday sermon (or *khuṭba*), in addition to other proclamations of faith. The content of *khuṭba* can vary, from commentaries on the Qur'ān to advice on common questions or issues. At all times, the imām projects authority in his proclamations. Many within his audience would respect his opinion (although this is perhaps not a universal factor in those listening to sermons!). An imām traditionally represented a central channel of communication within a community. They knew who the imām was, perhaps personally, depending on the size of the community. The community knew the extent of the imām's knowledge, and whether he had undertaken special training for his role, or was simply the 'best qualified' to lead prayers within a mosque.

In the age of the Internet, the *minbar* can be 'digital': concepts of community are changing along with forms of communication. The *khuṭba* can be online. Nobody need see the imām in order to follow him. He can be watched on the computer screen, replayed and analysed, his sermons transmitted globally either live or via recordings put on the web immediately after *Jum'a*, Friday prayers. Texts of sermons can be widely disseminated, projecting a theoretically universal authority.

Sermons can also be produced by anonymous sources, and, given that any individual or organization with the appropriate computer hardware, software and access to a service provider can produce an 'authoritative' Islamic website, traditional notions of religious authority can be circumnavigated in a computer-mediated environment. Authors' affiliations, locations and religious perspectives can be cloaked in online anonymity and can also be surfed anonymously.

Cyber Islamic Environments are produced in a variety of contexts, from a spectrum of Islamic perspectives and affiliations. A site's author can as easily be an individual as a transglobal organization. Given this diversity, it is possible to return to the question of whether there is a 'global electronic *umma*' online? Certainly there is a 'connectiveness' in certain areas of interest, and if the concept of *umma* relates to shared concepts, values and language with a single Muslim community, then at least superficially an argument could be made for the existence of this electronic *umma*. Clearly there can be significant differences in approaches to Islam *between* these sites, and evidence indicates that the web as a medium can be applied as a tool of censure and criticism between and within specific Muslim interests.

Phenomenologically, it is possible to locate that which is conceptually 'shared' between these sites. The paradigm of the so-called 'five pillars' of Islam (*arkān al-Islam*) is one that lends itself to an electronic 'connectiveness'. These all form part of the electronic landscape and dialogue: the principles of proclaiming a belief in One God whose Final Prophet was Muḥammad (*shahāda*); prayer (*ṣalāt*); fasting in Ramaḍān (*ṣawm*); an alms taxation (*zakāt*); and pilgrimage (*ḥajj*) are conceptually identified as 'similars' in these websites, even if their methodological fulfilment varies.

These commonalities can be located in dedicated websites – but they can also indicate *difference*. Take the example of prayer: guidance on how to pray is contained in several sites. Variations in approach to prayer do emerge within a global context, and some might find aspects that do not conform to their interpretation of appropriate practice. For example, the Online Islamic Propagation Team provides an extensive site detailing every step of prayer, together with audio clips of prayers explaining meaning and pronunciation. Surfers can click on an icon to hear and practise recitation of each prayer portion, and see illustrations of the positions within each prayer unit (*rak'a*).[1] This represents a considerable investment in time and technology for the purposes of propagation of Islam, and in general principle its methodological approach to prayer might be 'universal'. However, variables do emerge in different Muslim contexts and cultural settings, both between and within the broad (and potentially interchangeable) categories of Sunnī, Shī'a, and Ṣūfī Islam.

Similarly issues emerge on CyberSalat, a site which provides a sophisticated 'freeware' programme to teach prayer, which can be downloaded from its webpages.[2] There is no charge for this, although the user is invited to make a donation to a Muslim charity. CyberSalat describes itself as providing:

- Precise, step-by-step instructions in English.
- Accurate audio renditions of the Qur'an.
- Arabic text.
- English translation and transliteration.
- Colour graphics showing changes in postures required for prayer.
- Recitation of the *azan* (call to prayer).
- Recitation of eleven chapters from the Qur'ān.
- On-line context-sensitive help system.
- Easy-to-use and customizable interface.[3]

Simulations of prayer, together with appropriate 'real-time' recitations on sound files, make CyberSalat a technological leap forward in terms of free, accessible information on a pillar of Islam. Such a site also plays a *da'wa* role, in terms of potentially enhancing the knowledge of Islamic practice in such a practical way. It could be a useful resource to converts, as well as Muslims seeking to revive or enhance their religious practices. Variations relating to prayer time are also incorporated within the programme, providing a sense of depth of information in a user-friendly interface. Future editions will improve the Arabic font and audio files.[4] As a method of personal instruction, this could be one area in which the Internet becomes very effective propagation tool. The site also forms part of the Islamic Gateway, which, as discussed earlier, has a number of controversial links. The extent to which the development of CyberSalat encourages surfers to explore other links on the same pages is certainly one to consider.

The creator of CyberSalat, Monzur Aḥmed, has also identified Ramaḍān as another 'pillar' for the development of shared resources. Whilst the theme is not unique, much of the material is especially created for the site. Aḥmed has created extensive information resources on important aspects of the fasting month.[5] Especially relevant are co-ordinated data on the sighting of the new moon, which historically has been a source of controversy. Different regions and authorities have asserted independent views as to when *'Īd al-Fiṭr* (the concluding feast of Ramaḍān) should be celebrated. These differences of opinion are based on *how* moon sightings are calculated. The result has been that the *'Īd* has been celebrated at different times, even within the same geographical and cultural context, with different interpretations being followed in various mosques.

An attempt to clarify this issue scientifically has been made on this site, which contains a variety of Islamic and scientific resources for individuals (or community leaders) to make their own calculations, rather than simply pronouncing a date and time for *'Īd.* As the moon needs to be sighted to make a calculation, astronomy resources such as an Islamic calendar based on predicted moon sighting are integrated into the site's format. Links are provided to the Royal Greenwich Observatory site and the Jordanian Astronomical Society, the latter discussing the complex mathematical and theoretical basis for moon sighting.

It would be interesting to determine the extent to which such sites might influence decision-making on the moon-sighting issue. In the contemporary context, there are precedents for information on moon sighting to be transmitted globally to branches of an Islamic network by telephone or fax. Decisions can now also be e-mailed, if they are not calculated by individual communities, utilizing the scientific methods outlined above. Decisions can also now be accessed through browsing Cyber Islamic Environments. This could be another indicator of how the Internet could transcend traditional networks of authority whilst also creating a uniformity within an electronic *umma*.

Many other websites seek to project an Islamic authority in decision-making contexts, and there are several examples of digital advice to specific questions being available on the Internet. The intended audience can clearly only be those who are directly connected to the service, either through a mailing list, or through logging onto a site. Factors relating to confidentiality and 'Islamic authority' on the Internet have to be considered in the light of these recent technological developments. A single question or query for information would receive several different answers, depending upon which Muslim site was consulted. These sites may offer a database of previous questions, together with opportunities to e-mail 'experts' for consideration of a reply. These sites are often linked to e-mail lists, which further circulate opinions.

Often sites are searchable (within their own frameworks), although the development of a 'universal' search-engine or portal for a digital *umma* could extend opportunities for specific answers to be provided from diverse sources. This could be in the form of a search-engine, an equivalent of 'Ask Jeeves', in which a question might be entered.[6] In the interests of research, the writer entered a question about a common Islamic topic to 'Jeeves'. Given that this is a universal search-engine, not designed for 'Islamic' questions only, the response was effective. The question 'Which foods are ḥalāl?' was submitted to the search-engine. The listing of Jeeves's responses was headed by a link to the 'Guide to halal food selection', containing interpretative concerns relating to appropriate food products, based on Qur'ānic sources.[7]

A number of 'Islamic search-engines' have now been developed in specific contexts. For example, Islamic Finder searches for mosques in the United States.[8] There are also internal search-engines to search Islamic texts, including some of the primary sources discussed earlier. A wider example of a Muslim search-engine is that provided by Muslims Online, which searches its own database and other search-engines to obtain material. The test question on information about *ḥalāl* food resulted in twenty-two diverse links emerging.[9]

To extend questions about decision-making further, there are specific databases on the Internet containing advice from various 'authorities'. Whilst a proportion of this advice is contained in the form of sermons often available in other media forms, certain information is especially geared to the Internet, often through the form of searchable indexes created for the electronic medium. One example is located in Arabic-language cyberspace: a series of short sermons by Sheikh Said Sha'aban of Lebanon (d. June 1998 – the event was widely reported on various Islam-related sites) is available on a site, together with promised material from other authorities, and pages on Islamic Affairs.[10] This site was set up by Al-Moukhtar, an organization that was previously an Islamic radio and television broadcasting station in the north of Lebanon, '. . . but under some circumstances, we were obliged to close them both . . .'[11] Al-Moukhtar plans to circumvent these 'circumstances' of control over radio and television transmissions, which were probably in the form of local authorities in Lebanon disagreeing with their ethos. The organization intends to take advantage of the Internet to expand their services into live radio and TV broadcasting 'to continue spreading Islam all around the globe in a modern way, no matter what the costs are'.[12]

Sermon reproduction is becoming a feature of Cyber Islamic Environments, and examples can be found in many sites previously discussed. Some of these sermons project governmental views, or perspectives from other political standpoints. Some specialized advocates of *da'wa* have integrated the Internet within their wider propagation of Islam. One example is that of the Aḥmed Deedat, a South African Muslim preacher (*sic*) whose sermons and debates include subjects such as 'Jesus in Islam', 'Muhammad in the Bible', and a 'Combat Kit against Bible Thumpers', including audio versions.[13] Deedat additionally produces his *da'wa* message in print, video and cassette formats, all of which can be ordered online through the website. Deedat's particular focus is engaging in debate with Christians, in order to 'convert' or 'revert' Christians to Islam. Documentation includes Deedat's attempt to engage the Pope in a debate in the Vatican:

> It is acknowledged that the present Pope is a master psychologist, the shrewdest, the most popular and the most diplomatic of all Popes in Christendom.
>
> He makes everyone happy. On every foreign soil he lands, he kisses the ground – he makes SOOJOOD, the prostration (the climax in the Muslim prayer) – only a step away from the KALIMA, the creed (the Muslim declaration of Faith). This makes the Muslim very happy too.[14]

Deedat comments on other contemporary issues and social concerns, ranging from the Rushdie controversy to alcoholism. These populist themes combine with Deedat's rhetorical skills, and are contained in audio files that can be downloaded by surfers. They provide a sense of authority and leadership, are directed to a global (English-speaking) audience, and are outside the bounds of political and/or governmental frameworks. They are also a response to Christian–Muslim 'dialogues', given that there are numerous propagation pages in which advocates of particular perspectives argue their views.

The Internet caters for many interests relating to particular aspects of Islam or Muslim life. Whilst the decision-making sites emerging from the United States may be amongst those that are developmentally the most sophisticated, there are a number of other sites emerging from a variety of contexts. One with significant potential that emerged from Middle Eastern Muslim contexts is Yūsuf Qarādawī's Internet Pages, at the time of writing still 'under construction' by its Qatari authors(s). Qarādawī is seen as an important contemporary interpreter of Islamic issues, influential within a global context, especially in the field of decision-making. However, at the time of writing, the site was insufficiently developed for evaluation.[15]

Information about specific scholars and their approaches is located online, notably those associated with one of the most prestigious institutions of Muslim scholarship, Al-Azhar University in Cairo. During 1998, the institution was planning its own official site. An 'unofficial' Al-Azhar site also emerged, which detailed the lives of many of Al-Azhar's important graduates over a broad historical period; it also contained searchable indexes listing over a hundred scholars, together with subject indexes, a place-of-birth index and a chronological index. This is still in the developmental stage but suggests a potential future resource for individuals seeking information and advice on particular academic perspectives influenced by the Sunnī viewpoint of Al-Azhar.[16] An official Al-Azhar site containing information in Arabic and English emerged online during 1998, although its content was limited to a brief history and contact details.[17]

## 5.2 'Doubt and confusion': questions online

Authority in the form of questions and answers about Islam, allowing the individual surfer to post a query to an 'authority' by e-mail, also comprise part of Cyber Islamic Environments. Unlike sermons, these allow an element of participation and interactivity for users. One long-standing site offering this service is the Shī'a Ahlul Bayt 'Aalim Network, founded in 1995, and organized by volunteers:

> The main motivation for this site was for it to serve in replying to questions followers of the Shia school of thought have in their daily lives. It is also meant to educate all Muslims and non-Muslims about the Ja'ffari school of thought.
>
> Since this is a question and answer mailing list, our interaction is with those who submit questions. The questions are referred to scholars on the panel and the reply posted on the mailing list. Alhamdullilah, the site has been overwhelmingly well received.
>
> Over the next few years, it is likely that this site will remain in its present format with the hopes of having the material in the archives translated in different languages in order to benefit a wider audience.[18]

Questions and responses are categorized by subject, date and moderator. An archive is accessible via a search-engine. For example, a typical search provided twenty opinions for the term *ḥalāl*, including references to mushrooms, seafood, gelatine, genetic engineering, and eating where alcohol is served.[19]

The Ahlul Bayt 'Aalim Network e-mailing list material also provides a fascinating cross-section of questions, posted at regular intervals. Between June and November 1998, over two hundred answers were posted automatically to those on an e-mail list, reflecting contemporary concerns amongst this Shī'a community in North America, but also a readership beyond geographical and political frontiers. Concerns are very broad, given some of the less mainstream questions incorporated on the site. These include:

- the 'acceptability' of *mut'a* ('temporary marriage') with a prostitute (*forbidden*);
- how to deal with 'inappropriate behaviour in a mosque' (*negotiate*);
- 'how can I become a *mujtahid* [in this context, an interpreter of Muslim law]?' (*study*);
- 'dry cleaning and prayers';
- a question on the 'acceptability' of homosexuality and gender change (*not acceptable*).[20]

However, the majority of questions are rather more traditional, relating to prayer, practice and obligation. Each answer provides some insight into the formulation of opinions by these particular

Shīʿa authorities, and also into concerns in the minority context of the United States. The answers frequently follow a specific formula, citing Islamic primary sources and precedent, as this edited example demonstrates:

> In the Name of Allah, the Compassionate, the All-Merciful, Greeting of Allah be upon Muhammad and the pure members of his House
>
> Salamun alaykum
>
> The reply to the following question was kindly provided by Shaykh Rasheed.
>
> Wasalaam,
>
> Mustafa Rawji
> Moderator, Aalim Network
>
> QUESTION:
>
> Most of my friends are not of the Shia faith and many times they ask me 'practical' questions which I cannot answer. For example, they asked me why I am not allowed to wear gold and why is it forbidden to keep dogs as pets (why are they haram [forbidden]).
>
> As a Shia, I tell them that the only things I should question are about the oneness of God and about the prophethood of Mohammed (a.s.). Once I have accepted these things then I should follow the teachings without question. That is not say that I don't seek out the answers or the reasons, but I also accept that Allah knows much more than I. However, these are usually not satisfactory answers.
>
> Please give me the answers to the above question and also some reference books so that I may look up and answer these questions myself
>
> ANSWER:
>
> Wa Alaikum As-Salaam,
>
> The Prophet Muhammad (S) prohibited the men of his followers from wearing gold and prohibited all Muslims from using gold as utensils for eating and drinking. It is generally understood that one of the main reasons for this is that gold was usually used in those times as jewellery for the very wealthy and powerful who adorned

themselves as a show of wealth and/or power. It was usually the rulers who wore gold and used it as utensils. It was also usually the case that they acquired their wealth by force, oppression and corruption. The Holy Prophet (S) refused such things for himself and others even when they were only symbolically connected with unjust rulers and oppression.

It can be seen in the incident of Mubahilah when the Christian leaders first appeared to meet with out Holy Prophet (S), he observed how lavishly they were adorned with gold. He refused to meet with them until they removed these embellishments which he complained was inconsistent with piety and godly men.

With regards to dogs, there are two animals which the Shari'ah has not only forbidden its consumption but ruled it as impure. They are the dog and pig.

To make a long story short. Allah Ta'ala has turned disobedient and sinful people into these animals as a punishment. This is mentioned in the Torah and Islamic traditions. The Quran mentions that man was turned into apes in a similar manner. Due to this, these animals have a specific status in Islamic Law.

Unfortunately, there are not adequate reference books in English that I could refer that you might find these answers yourself. They exist in Arabic and Persian and perhaps Urdu. You mentioned that after belief you should follow without question. I personally disagree. You should ask questions which strengthen your understanding and belief. You should avoid such questions that cause doubt and confusion in your mind.

Was-Salaam,

Ali Rasheed.[21]

The questions to the network are frequently anonymous. Each is individually answered, placed within the Internet archive, and e-mailed to list members. The formulation of opinion is based on Islamic primary sources and, in this context, the authority of Shīʿa sources as well (where appropriate). The moderator and scholars utilize different language sources to reach a conclusion (when possible) or to produce advice. Within the site, the formulae of responses incorporate Islamic salutations and terms (where appropriate). Twentieth-century scholars cited include Āyatullāh Khameneʿī, Āyatullāh Seestanī, Āyatullāh Khoei and

Āyatullāh Khumaynī. The network's format resembles printed scholastic and advice sources available elsewhere. In terms of a networking model, the 'Aalim Network site demonstrates the potential at least for a sector within the Shī'a spectrum, given that questions are real concerns to individuals located in different contexts throughout the digital world. This is also a model that might be reproduced elsewhere, or developed further in terms of interactivity, given appropriate resources.

A similar service is offered by the Islamic Assembly of North America (IANA), which provides a direct link to their 'Fatwa and Research Centre', whose 'knowledgeable Sheikhs and students of knowledge will answer questions' by e-mail. The perspective of this service is different from 'Aalim Network, emerging from an Ahl al-Sunnah wa 'l-Jamā'a Sunnī background.[22]

Another American-based service is Ask the Imam, organized through the IslamiCity site, which is supported by membership subscription (although open to all surfers). Scholars from Beirut, Florida and California are listed as the authorities, and an e-mail can be forwarded to them.[23] The introduction to the site states that: 'The answers to the questions may only reflect the opinions of the scholars; they are not necessarily "fatwas". The management of this site does not necessarily endorse these opinions.'[24]

The site has a searchable index of more than 4,000 questions, on a variety of topics. Again these represent the diverse interests of Muslims, not just in North America, but elsewhere. These include the 'obscure' issues as well as the mainstream, ranging from credit-card use to meeting women on the Internet. Many of the listed questions appear unanswered on the database (this is potentially frustrating for surfers seeking solutions to their questions). Given the content of the questions submitted, they do not appear to be 'moderated'. However, a search for a broad topic such as *ḥalāl* brings up diverse questions and responses, indicative of the IslamiCity site's agenda, as the following edited extract suggests:

> Question: As-salamo-alaikum, What is Islamic view on Listening Music and dating?
>
> Answer: As-salaamu alaykum. The issue of Music has been an issue of debate and disagreement between Muslim scholars. Some of them

view it as Halal, other ones view it as Haram. We will give here the opinion of Dr Yusuf al-Qaradawi:

> Among the entertainments which may comfort the soul, please the heart, and refresh the ear is singing. Islam permits singing under the condition that it not be in any way obscene or harmful to Islamic morals. There is no harm in its being accompanied by music which is not exciting. In order to create an atmosphere of joy and happiness, singing is recommended on festive occasions such as the days of 'Eid, weddings and wedding feasts, births, 'aqiqat (the celebration of the birth of a baby by the slaughter of sheep), and on the return of a traveler. 'Aishah narrated that when a woman was married to an Ansari man, the Prophet (peace be on him) said, ' 'Aishah, did they have any entertainment? The Ansar are fond of entertainment.' (Reported by al-Bukhari.) . . .

[several other *aḥādīth* follow]

> . . . However, since singing is in many cases associated with drinking parties and night clubs, many scholars have declared it to be haram or at least makruh. They state that singing constitutes that kind of idle talk which is mentioned in the ayah, And among the people is the one who buys idle talk (at the expense of his soul) in order to lead (people) astray from the path of Allah without knowledge, holding it in mockery; for such there will be a humiliating punishment. (31:6) . . .

[citations from the Qur'ān and other commentators follow]

> . . . As to the issue of dating it is forbidden in Islam for many reasons and Muslims take pride of not dating because it preserves the sanctity, dignity, respect, and chastity of the human being. Any person would agree that if dating was not so common nowadays, then, our society wouldn't be experiencing so many problems with teenage pregnancies, children left abandoned to orphanages or foster homes, single parenthood and so on. In addition, even if dating didn't involve sexual relations, all the acts that dating may lead a couple to do, such [as] being alone in secluded areas, touching, kissing, etc. between non-married couples are prohibited and condemned in Islam. As you know, Islam encourages marriage, ethical behaviour, and the preservation of the family, and dating contradicts with one or all of these goals. A couple who dates is not bound to get married, and this wastes the time of one or both of them to establish a family. Also, social studies have proved

> that dating, which some people claim is necessary for a couple to know each other before marriage, doesn't lead to happier and more successful marriages. Actually, in many countries where dating is the highest in the world, divorce rate is also the highest. But this doesn't mean that a Muslim couple who wants to get married doesn't have the right to know each other. Instead, while getting to know each other, the adult couple has to be in the presence of other people and never in seclusion. The couple has to respect the Islamic guidelines, and both of them have to realize that they are together for the purpose of getting married in the future and not for having fun. Also, since dating may lead to committing fornication, God had warned us in many verses in the Qur'an from approaching it. This is confirmed in many verses such as in Surah al-Isra' (17) Verse 32; Surah an-Nour (24) verses 2–3; Surah al-Furqan (25) verse 68; Surah al-Mumtahina (60) verse 12. Thank you for asking and God knows best.[25]

Again, this illustrates a decision-making formula, and a model of online authority, including an opinion from the important contemporary interpreter, Yūsuf Qarādawī (discussed above). Within the full text, there is also a hyperlink to another website, providing further information. This could be described as one 'Sunnī' perspective online, representing a 'orthodox' pattern of interpretation, based on Qur'ān, *aḥādīth* and *fiqh* (jurisprudence) sources. Amidst this material, there are responses to contemporary issues in the USA, and a social-scientific justification for not 'dating'. This type of response might encourage other surfers to present their questions.

Other responses within the site suggest that many of those seeking advice also require some form of counselling as well as 'Islamic advice', especially on questions relating to divorce. This reflects views expressed to this writer during other fieldwork research, where decision-makers felt that many of the questions they received were cries for help rather than issues of interpretation.[26] The Internet currently provides an extra dimension to this, with its provision of anonymity (although the technical potential to trace e-mail exists in some contexts):

> Question: I am going through a trial separation with my wife of 2.5 years and I'm very confused about what I should do next. I've made Dua [extra prayer] and read Salaah [prayer] but my head and my heart conflict on what my decision should be. I need advice.

Answer: Dear Br. Z. [Brother Z] As-salaamu alaykum. What you are going through is normal because divorce is one of the most traumatic experiences a person can have. Try to reach a stage of peace within yourself, turn to God, and start building a new life. However, although divorce is very difficult, it is not the end of the world and therefore, you shouldn't stop all of your life activities. Also, during this difficult period of time, you may be considering to go back and remarry your old wife. This is of course an alternative that you should consider in case rebuilding the relationship with her has a viable prospect for long-term success. In any case, never lose trust in God and have hope that the situation will improve in the near future. Thank you for asking and God knows best.[27]

The significant number of hits that IslamiCity receives would indicate that the advice/authority dimensions of the site are accessed by a large number of people. However, how qualified the authorities might be in terms of some of the questions, which enter the zone of the psychological damage that individual questioners might have suffered, is open to question. One question in this area addressed suicide and homosexuality:

Question: Dear Imam, Salamu Alaikum, I fear Allah, and believe in him so strongly that I cry when I pray . . . My problem is homosexuality. Believe me Sir that I pray to Allah that I am dead for having these uncontrollable feelings, I do not want to be gay, I try to change, but all this seem to be beyond my capability. For many years I've prayed to Allah to correct me, I really prayed very Sincerely with a clean heart, but I am only the same since I was a young boy . . . If I ever commit an act with another man, should not I be killed? I must admit, I have, and I wish I am dead. In such a situation, (and since we do not live in a Muslim state where islamic law should be upheld) should I not kill myself and therefore upholding the law and MAY BE getting forgiveness from Allah.. I know suicide is not allowed, but in a case like mine, and being well aware of some Islamic laws, shouldn't we have an exception and allow suicide? I really fear Allah alot and I can not help my uncontrollable feelings, Allah knows best that I submit to Him, and willing to do anything for forgiveness from my grave sin . . . Please respond asap [as soon as possible] . . . Thank you Sirs . . .

Answer: Dear Br. [brother] As-salaamu alaykum. Two wrongs don't make one right. While homosexuality is wrong, it doesn't justify

> suicide under any conditions or circumstances. Please know that if you ever commit suicide, you would have seriously misunderstood Islam and its spirit. What you should do is to truly repent to Allah, The Merciful, The Gracious, and pledge to Him never to get involved in any homosexual acts anymore. If medical or psychological counselling helps, then get it, but know that Allah is The Curer, and the Qur'an is your best companion. Give charity, pray, make dua' [supererogatory prayer or invocation], and Allah will not leave you alone. You have got to believe in the infinite amount of Mercy Allah provides to His servants, and you should also realize that He forgives, if He wishes, all types of sins, except the sin of disbelieving in Him. Therefore, don't lose hope in Him and write us anytime you want. Thank you for asking and God knows best.[28]

It would seem that Cyber Islamic Environments allow sensitive questions of this kind to be addressed, which would be unsuitable or impossible in other circumstances. In terms of their 'acceptability', it is highly unlikely that certain other Muslim platforms would sympathize with the questioner in this way. For example, if the Taliban Online were to address this issue, it is highly unlikely that they would reach the same conclusion. This perhaps indicates the boundaries of a digital *umma*, ranging from shared concerns such as prayer to contentious issues of ethics, morals and interpretation.

To take this issue a stage further, the Internet also contains sites that are written by and cater for gay, lesbian and bisexual people who describe themselves as Muslim. Queer Jihad, run by Sulayman X, attempts to reconcile gay and Muslim identities. The site publishes its e-mail feedback on a regular basis, and the balance seems to be generally between those sending messages abusing the site (and its readers) and those broadly sympathetic.[29] Queer Jihad also lists a broad range of sympathetic sites elsewhere on the Internet. A related site also advertises a mailing list for 'Muslim Homosexuals', together with links for 'transgendered women', lesbians, and gay men.[30] Questions emerge as to whether these sites can be incorporated within the term Cyber Islamic Environments. Many perspectives would not ascribe that identity to them, given their negative appraisal of sexual relations outside marriage and of homosexuality.

Controversial issues also appear on another decision-making database archive contained on the IslamiCity site, which extensively reproduces opinions in a searchable index format from the *Arab News*, Jeddah.[31] Again this introduces a broad range of topics, illustrating contemporary concerns as well as questions based around primary issues of interpretation. The difference here is that opinions are presented from Saudi Arabia, which promotes itself as a centre of Sunnī 'orthodoxy'. There are, for example, at least sixty-two references on aspects of fasting; 193 relating to prayer; sixty-eight on *zakāt*; and seventy-two on *ḥajj*. Many of the responses on family law again indicate questions which might be difficult to address in other contexts. For example:

> Question: Some old men in their seventies marry young girls who are still in their early twenties or younger. Do you think that there is some injustice done to such young women? Is there any remedy to such a situation?
>
> Answer: There is certainly much injustice if the girl is forced to accept such a marriage. It does happen that a wealthy old man proposes to a young woman and her family review the marriage as a method which could rid them of their poverty. They persuade or force their daughter to accept the marriage caring very little for her feelings or her future. If the case is such, then it is a case of blatant injustice and it should be stopped. On the other hand, if the girl goes into such a marriage with open eyes and with full agreement, then the marriage is simply a contract between two competent persons. Since it is a contract to something which is halal or permissible in Islam, it is perfectly permissible. It may be that the girl goes into such a marriage hoping to have a good share of the inheritance of her husband. This does not disallow or invalidate the marriage, because neither she nor anyone else could tell how soon the man would die. It is perfectly possible that she dies before him. The remedy to such a situation is the full implementation of Islam, which means that no family should live in a standard of poverty which compels it to marry away its girls to rich old people to improve their situation. In Islam, the system of social security ensures that.[32]

Such questions raise important social issues, which many communities and individuals seek to address. It has particular relevance in the context in which the question originally emerged (in the pages of *Arab News*, Jeddah). The religion editor seeks to analyse these questions in the light of his understanding of *shar'īa*, and there is no guarantee that his response would be appreciated in other contexts. Again the Internet provides an 'anonymous' arena in which social concerns can be addressed and examined.

For example, it is unlikely that the following question could safely be asked within certain Muslim contexts:

> Question: If a couple begets a child illegitimately, what is to be done?
>
> Answer: In a state in which Islamic law is applied, the pregnancy of an unmarried woman is an undeniable evidence of adultery [unless a case of rape has earlier been reported by the woman] which is punishable in Islam. The punishment is the same for both man and woman. No blame is attached to the child as the result of his parents' sin. Any person who is guilty of fornication or adultery should repent his or her sin and pray to Allah to forgive him or her. An order that applies to all sins is that the perpetrator should not publicize his action. This also applies in this case. If an adulterer confesses to his guilt or if four witnesses testify to having seen him doing it, the punishment described by Islam is enforceable. However, if the couple get married when the pregnancy becomes evident, and try to keep their affair secret, they do well, especially if they repent having committed this sin. They may hope to be forgiven by Allah. If the father admits that the child is his own, his admission is accepted and he is not questioned with regard to the time of pregnancy and whether it was a legitimate one or not.[33]

Whilst this response conforms to a particular *madhhab* or school of interpretation, there are few other Cyber Islamic Environments in which it is addressed in such practical terms. No specific sources are mentioned in terms of precedents or consensus of opinions in relation to this issue: the subtext is that the reader should accept the opinion without challenge. The impact of such sites on the Internet needs to be analysed in more detail, as other decision-making frameworks come online. As a means of education and information, as well as practical advice on Islam, they add another dimension to forms of Muslim computer-mediated communication online, especially given their interactive component and their potential anonymity.

A similar database of Shaykh Dr ad-Darsh's discussions on Islamic interpretation, originally contained in the *Q-News* magazine produced in London, is now available on the Belfast

Islamic Centre site. Darsh contributed his column 'What you ought to know' over a five-year period prior to his death in 1997, and answered questions on a broad range of themes. The Internet version contains a cross-section of responses (from 1996–7 issues) which illustrate the concerns of a selection of Muslims in the United Kingdom. These include reconciling Islamic practices with living in a minority context, and also evaluating the appropriate application of 'technology'. For example, Darsh's column contained references to developments in medical technology, such as organ transplantation, *in vitro* fertilization and euthanasia. The following question is an example of one of these concerns:[34]

> Question: Is there anything wrong with me having an ultrasound scan to determine the sex of my unborn baby?
>
> Answer: There is no objection from the Islamic Shari'ah in having an ultrasound scan to know the sex of the unborn baby as long as it is a matter of knowledge about the baby. But I am afraid there may have been here a hidden motive. Some people prefer to have, say, a male child, and they use ultrasound to determine the sex. If what they learn is not according to their liking, they will terminate the pregnancy. This is totally unacceptable from the Islamic point of view. But if it is only a matter of knowing the sex of the child there is no problem in doing so.[35]

This clearly raises issues beyond the application of ultrasound technology and enters the cultural domain of preference for a male child and abortion of female babies, which can be issues of concern for sectors and individuals in Britain's Muslim (and non-Muslim!) population. Although published in *Q-News*, the Darsh column in collected form is not officially available in formats other than the Internet.

Amongst the many themes contained in the columns, the issue of converts was one that frequently featured in Darsh's columns, especially in terms of 'values' and approaches towards these newcomers to Islam. Given that *da'wa* or propagation is seen as an obligation, and that it features strongly in many Cyber Islamic Environments, the following question is useful to consider. This is not just in the immediate context of the 'local mosque' discussed, but perhaps as an analogy for broader issues connected with the Internet:

> Question: After Eid prayers at my local mosque, I saw a bewildered looking Englishman looking confused and not knowing how to fit into the atmosphere of Eid celebrations around him. I later found out that he'd become a Muslim that very day, but did not know where to go or what to do. Surely he deserved better treatment. What is the responsibility of the community on new Muslims?
>
> Answer: Islamically-speaking, the responsibility if the community on new Muslims is great. Unfortunately we have until now not been able to set up institutions or procedures for fully implementing them. This explains the sad spectacle you have observed.
>
> One of the reasons for this deficiency is the relatively low priority the community has given to the responsibility. This has to change. For new Muslims, merely reciting the words of the Shahadah is not sufficient, he needs both knowledge about Islam and a social context to practise it. Of course this in turn needs money and trained personnel, something which has been in short supply. But it'll always be in short supply so there's no use in complaining. We have to make a start somewhere sometime. Such trained personnel have to look after the needs of new Muslim adults and their young children.
>
> Remember these children, like our own children, have experienced nothing but the norms and attitudes of the West. They more than anyone need practical demonstrations of moral and spiritual values. It is simply no good to lock them up and hope that somehow, divorced from the world, they will miraculously become good Muslims. They have to be gently guided through the transition from their familiar old environment into their new communities and families.[36]

This need to assist newcomers has been identified on the Internet, with the provision of specific sites for converts. These seek to answer questions for newcomers (and perhaps encourage others to convert to Islam). A good example of this is ConvertsToIslam, a site hosted in the United States; this site is connected with a daily e-mailing list, and other sites produced by the same author. This site is regularly updated, and caters for a niche audience through the provision of accessible material written by other, more 'experienced' converts. For example, it links into practical advice from converts at another site on how a convert should inform her or his family about 'conversion':

> Before you decide to announce your reversion to loved ones who are non-Muslim, make sure you are ready for their response, whether it is pleasant or horrible. Being ready means many things: understanding

> the basics of practicing your faith, understanding the reasons behind actions demanded of you by Islam, and being able to reconcile unfortunate world events that are attributed to Muslims with your own understanding of Islam and its inherent goodness, logic, and beauty.
>
> As hypocritical as it may be, many open-minded people cease to be open-minded when difficult issues such as religious conversion 'hit home.' People who are ordinarily rational, educated, and worldly unfortunately can swing 180 degrees when a person they love converts to a religion they do not appreciate or understand. It may be in your best interest, and in theirs, to not discuss your reversion to Islam until a year or two has passed and you feel comfortable in your faith. At that point, it would be obvious to them that Islam has not made you a worse or lesser person, and has in fact (hopefully!) noticeably improved you![37]

As a support system for converts or 'reverts', especially in dispersed contexts, the Internet provides opportunities that can only increase, as the technology becomes cheaper and more accessible. The ConvertsToIslam site is particularly interesting, because of the assumptions it makes regarding converts: that they will all be Sunnī, perhaps following beliefs geared exclusively around the Qur'ān and Sunna, with little or no interest in the esoteric dimensions of Islam, focused on legal prescription. Converts adhering to other branches of Sunnī Islam, or Shī'a Islam, are not catered for in this site. Whilst stressing the 'tolerant' nature of Islam, ConvertsToIslam also links into sites that are less than favourable to some of these other aspects of Islam, such as anti-Aḥmadiyyah sites. This is at a time where individual new converts might be impressionable to political and other agendas.

## 5.3 Dialogue and authority online: 'SuraLikeIt'

The issue of conversion is an important one, given that a number of sites focus upon propagation materials, in an attempt to attract surfers to (their own particular understanding of) Islam. The polemical aspects of sectors within the Internet mean that sites are often utilized to denounce rival belief-systems, or to 'answer' the questions one belief raises about another. The extent to which these sites are preaching to the converted needs to be considered, or whether they would be utilized by those seeking balanced debates on the subject. Whilst inter-faith dialogue might suggest mutual toleration between different religious beliefs, a number of sites only seek converts, not tolerance. Rivals are condemned. Many seek to project themselves as the authentic, definitive voice of their belief-system.

A large number of Muslim sites have appeared to counter what they perceive to be 'aggressive' Christian sites. Many of these sites are well-stocked with articles with titles such as 'What do Muslims think of Jesus?', 'Did Jesus and Isaiah prophesy the coming of Muhammad?', '101 Contradictions in the Bible', and 'The Trinity Exposed'.[38] It is not the intention here to enter into the detailed polemical dimensions of these sites and pages, which assert clear positions relating to their own self-perception and identities online. A certain amount of this particular material also features in print form. One extensive Muslim Internet reaction to Christianity is Answering Christianity, organized by the author of ConvertsToIslam, Shawn Smith. This identifies its target as being those Christians who are not 'respectful' to Islam:

> As you surf the Internet you will quickly realize that there are several Christian web sites which are targeted towards Muslims. For the most part they are very aggressive and their sole purpose is to instil doubts in the Muslim's heart as to the truth of Islam and that only Christianity is the path to salvation. In fact there is one group that calls itself Aggressive Christianity. This group has some especially hateful things to say about Islam. Also, many other Christian groups are openly practising deception towards unwary Muslims and we need to become aware.
>
> . . . These distortions are purposely being promoted, not for the sake of an honest search for truth, but to maliciously attack the character of the prophet and the beauty of Islam. Nonetheless, there is a lot of effort taking place on the Internet to help clear up many Christian distortions and misconceptions about Islam.[39]

Whether this effort is simply the same type of rhetoric in reverse, *or* something that genuinely assists in the clarification of Islam, is open to question. The choice of the title Answering Christianity is itself combative, given that one of the 'aggressive' 'Christian' (*sic*?) sites has the title Answering Islam. The inter-faith webwars have developed to the extent that there are now sites with titles such as The Answer to Answering Islam.[40]

A number of 'Christian' sites attempt to analyse Islam and Muslims, proclaiming various levels of balance. Answering Islam, authored by Jochen Katz, is one of the most prominent, with hundreds of links to related Christian and Muslim sites.[41] The site is assertive with its position, criticizing Muslim sites that assume that atheist anti-Islam sites are 'Christian'. Answering Islam does not seek to present itself as 'apologetic': 'Our interest is the dialog and discussion with Muslims and the interaction with Islamic arguments on the basis of our common belief in God, the Creator and Sustainer of the Universe.' [42]

This dialogue is perhaps inexhaustible, given the substantial amount of polemical material produced by or linked to the Answering Islam site. Specific interpretations of Christianity and their responses to Islam need to be considered, as Answering Islam projects a quite specific understanding of Christianity. Further analysis of inter-religious dialogues might include Internet representation of Islam, not just from Muslims, but by followers of other belief-systems, where specific issues, dialogues and assumptions emerge. This is particularly pertinent when users of search-engines type in a key word such as 'Islam' or 'Muslim' and emerge with links to sites promoting other belief-systems (and making negative statements about Islam).[43]

Perhaps the most extreme example of a non-Muslim 'challenge' to Cyber Islamic Environments came from the SuraLikeIt website in 1998. This attempted to answer the following verse from the Qur'ān:

> And if ye are in doubt as to what We have revealed from time to time to Our servant then produce a Surah like thereunto; and call your witnesses or helpers (if there are any) besides Allah if your (doubts) are true.
>
> But if ye cannot and of a surety ye cannot then fear the fire whose fuel is Men and Stones which is prepared for those who reject Faith.[44]

It could also be a reaction to this *sūra*: 'Say: "If the whole of mankind and Jinns were to gather together to produce the like of this Qur'an they could not produce the like thereof even if they backed up each other with help and support." '[45]

In response to such *suwra* from the Qur'ān, the SuraLikeIt website produced four fabricated '*suwra*' entitled:

(a) *Surah al-Iman* (Faith)
(b) *Surah at-Tajassud* (the Incarnation)
(c) *Surah al-Muslimoon* (Muslims)
(d) *Surah al-Wasya* (Commandments).[46]

These '*suwra*' were produced in Arabic, English and transliterated formats, probably by a Christian Arab (or Arabs). There was an attempt to reproduce the metre and language from the Qur'ān, but they also had what could be described as a satirical edge to them as well, depending on the reader's perspective. Whilst Muslim reaction was primarily negative, there were other responses as well.

Samples from the '*suwra*' indicate their author(s)' interests (and targets). For example, '*al-Muslimoon*' states:

> (3) Those who disbelieved in God and his Christ shall have in the lifeafter the fire of hell and a severe torture.
>
> (7–9) They [the Muslims] said: We did not go astray ourselves but he, who claimed he was one of the messengers [of God] has misled us.
>
> (8) And as God says: O Muhammad, you allured my servants and caused them to become disbelieves [*sic*].
>
> (9) He said: O my Lord, it is Satan who allured me and truly he has always been the most corrupting to children of Adam.[47]

These negative statements suggest that the Qur'ān was a fabrication, and that Satan was involved in Muḥammad's attempt to 'mislead' and 'corrupt'. This is probably why the author(s) of these '*suwra*' retained anonymity.

Other verses include detailed references to the al-Bukhārī *Aḥādīth* collection, linking into the Muslim Students Association site to do so! The texts also include 'commandments' relating to marriage, personal hygiene and magic. The nature of Revelation is directly challenged. 'And when you [Muḥammad?] are short of commandments, call Jibril and he shall come in a hurry as he was ordered.'[48] The results of these pages appearing on the Internet introduce a range of complex issues, associated with censorship, freedom of information and the role of service providers.

A number of Muslim platforms attempted to have the pages removed from the Internet, and e-mail was used in order to mobilize a response. Media in the Middle East also picked up the issue, especially in Cairo, where it made the front pages of newspapers: perhaps in a response to this public protest, Al-Azhar University scholars launched a complaint in June 1998, led by their president Aḥmed Omar Hāshem: 'This is aggression on the human heritage and sacred values not only of Moslems, but of all humanity . . .'[49] Al-Azhar announced it would establish its own website, to counter such claims. Whilst there is now an 'official' Al-Azhar site (discussed above), at the time of writing, it was not fulfilling this agenda.[50]

Consideration was given by other platforms to suing SuraLike-It's Internet provider AOL (America On Line), although there was uncertainty on all sides regarding the legal position on such a move. A campaign to utilize e-mail and faxes to lobby AOL was launched by a number of groups, who also suggested that AOL's Muslim customers should change their Internet provider.

On 24 June 1998, AOL responded by closing down the SuraLikeIt pages, stating: 'We have removed that page. Our terms of service are very clear on what we call appropriate content, such as content which is defamatory in nature. This page had that. It was particularly targeting Islam.'[51] Some Muslim platforms perceived this as a 'victory' for a reasoned campaign rather than an 'overreaction' similar to that of the aftermath of the Salman Rushdie controversy (a sequence of events that took place prior to the mass utilization of the Internet). They believed it demonstrated the potential of e-mail as a lobbying tool.

One Muslim felt strongly enough to claim that the protests against SuraLikeIt would have negative implications for Muslim communities, and that the reactions had inadvertently given SuraLikeIt greater publicity:

> Consider this: the site does not claim to consist of suras from the Qur'an. There is nothing on the site which would make someone who does not know Arabic and Qur'an think that these were verses from the Qur'an, and one who does know Qur'an will immediately recognise that they are not Qur'anic verses . . .
>
> Then there are links to the individual 'suras' written by SuraLikeIt. Nowhere does the site say that these are verses from the Qur'an; in fact, anyone with a modicum of intelligence would immediately not infer that they are not, that they are attempts to imitate the Qur'an. And this would be correct.
>
> Now, are they successful attempts? A wave of protest about 'fake Qur'anic verses' will, essentially, confirm that the attempt was

> successful. I am certain that SuraLikeIt considers this protest . . . as a sign that he has been successful in imitating the Qur'an . . .
>
> . . . It is difficult for me to think of something which Muslims could do which would more meet the definition of 'saddun 'an sabiylillah,' blocking the path of God, than the kind of hysterical response which this protest represents. It massively discredits Islam and Muslims in the sight of the rest of the world – as well as among Muslims – and represents an abandonment of our responsibility to convey the message 'in the best of ways' . . .[52]

This commentator raises some important issues, especially the one of 'identifying' the '*suwra*' as fabrications. It could be suggested that in some cases the critics of SuraLikeIt did not read the full text (this has echoes of the Rushdie controversy). The 'anti-Islam' statements of the '*suwra*' are perhaps mild, compared with other sites on the web. On the other hand, the critics of SuraLikeIt exercised a legitimate right to make their comments. It would be interesting to see how much further they are prepared to go to criticize what they deem to be inappropriate material on the Internet, given that other sectors of the web contain materials that might be interpreted as far more detrimental to 'Muslim morality'.

Other Muslim critics of the reaction to SuraLikeIt included the United Submitters International (Submitters) based in Tucson, Arizona. This extensive website includes a lengthy commentary on the SuraLikeIt pages, suggesting that the reaction was simply 'ignorance':

> This kind of reaction by many of the traditional Muslims and the Muslim scholars, only reflects their ignorance with the Quran and the miracle of the Quran. It also reflects their inability to understand the Quran or follow its teachings . . .
>
> The reader of the Quran can easily recognize that, the challenge to produce a sura like it, is a genuine challenge by God, Almighty, the author of the Quran to all the humans and Jinn [ethereal beings, spirits]. It is meant to be taken seriously. Any human being alone or with the help of any force on earth is allowed to take it. For these Scholars and their followers to prevent the challenge from taking place is to stop the application of the Quran, as God wants it. This only reflects their own insecurity and their failure to trust in God, the author of the Quran . . .
>
> . . . Those scholars gave themselves the job of the bodyguards of the Quran, a job that was never trusted to them by God. Nor does God

> need their intervention to stop a challenge He issued over 1400 years ago.
>
> Actually those scholars and their followers do not differ much from the person who tried to meet the challenge and posted his 'Sura like it' pages. Both are ignorant with the true challenge in the Quran and the miracle of the Quran that makes it impossible to produce 'Sura like it' . . .[53]

The Submitters' pages go on to discuss how they perceive the Qur'ān as a mathematical miracle, and that without the mathematical underpinning, it is impossible even to produce a 'verse like it', let alone a *sūra*. The mathematical understanding is based on a complex sequence of factors, and the Submitters invited readers to meet the challenge through its pages.[54]

Inevitably, perhaps, given the nature of the Internet, SuraLikeIt's pages were reproduced elsewhere after being removed from AOL, under the title SuraLikeIt-UK. These pages also included an overview of the censorship issues, articles from the Arabic press, and a 'response' to the complaints. At the time of writing, SuraLikeIt's pages were still accessible online. They claim to acknowledge Muslim sensitivities, and try to respond to criticism of SuraLikeIt from another Internet source, IslamFirst, which took the position in terms of regarding SuraLikeIt as a gross insult:

> Those who see this case in the light of the freedom of expression as viewed and practiced in the West strongly argue for the right of a forger to write and express himself in which ever way he chooses while, on the other hand, there are those who regard his work as blasphemous and a clear violation of all noble principles.[55]

The Internet provides a platform for dialogues on issues of concern to Muslims from all sides. As can be seen from the SuraLikeIt issue, attempts at 'censorship' are not universally endorsed, and given the nature of the Internet are not always successful. It could be said that whilst it is easy for an individual to publish on the Internet an opinion about Islam, obtaining publicity for a site is more difficult. SuraLikeIt obtained a substantial number of hits, and was linked into sites such as Answering Islam prior to being taken off by AOL. After its re-instatement, locating the verses was relatively easy, given the application of an appropriate search-engine.[56] The republishers of SuraLikeIt noted that the censorship of the site could easily be applied to an 'unorthodox Islamic site'(*sic*).[57]

Questions arise of how the reader discerns 'authority' online, and what is classified as Islam and Islamic. The nature of Internet identity is different from other paradigms of identity. Anonymity of authors allows for expressions of 'being Muslim' that would not necessarily be feasible in the non-online world. Determining whether something is 'Qur'ān-ic', as in the case of SuraLikeIt, would seem an easier test. Although it *might* not have been the intention of SuraLikeIt to pretend to be 'genuine', some parties misread it as this.

Logically, to take SuraLikeIt one stage further, the potential exists for the creation of a totally fabricated 'Islam' site, containing unauthentic materials and opinions, and claiming to be the 'genuine article'. The potential also exists for different religious perspectives to 'hack' into each other's sites and paste messages representing their own opinions.[58] There may be issues of Muslim etiquette associated with whether hacking is 'permissible', together with potential for different perspectives within the Islamic spectrum to hack each other on the basis of *da'wa* activities. This is a development that should be monitored in further research on the topic.

## 5.4 Concluding comments

When considering authority online, perhaps the Internet should only be perceived as an adjunct to 'conventional wisdom'. During the 1990s, however, a number of 'authorities' and individuals assumed a status of moral and intellectual superiority in matters of religion, with the assumed ability to be able to 'guide' others. Whilst these views are acceptable to many, in time they may subvert and rival traditional channels of knowledge.

In terms of networking, the concept of an *umma* may have increased in feasibility (at least through digital networking) for some parties. If the ideal of the *umma* is that of a single network emerging from one 'server', then in theory the Internet could provide this for Muslims. Factors associated with accessibility, the type of surfer, and sheer divergence within understandings would suggest that in practice this would be impossible, or indeed not even an aspiration for many seeking to preserve their own understandings and interpretations. The Qur'ān itself recognized this potential for diversity, and it was something Muḥammad had to contend with throughout his prophetic period.

# 6

# *Cyber Islamic futures*

Cyber Islamic Environments offer insight into aspects of Islam, Muslim identities and issues associated with the 'Islamic' worlds. Computer-mediated communication provides a sense of commonality, associated with shared expressions and understandings, which might be described or associated with the concept of *umma*. The Internet also gives indications of the diversity associated with these Muslim expressions and understandings.

This is not the full picture as far as contemporary Islam goes. Many sectors, platforms and perspectives do not have, and may not wish to have, a presence online. The nature of computer-mediated communication suggests that it is the educated élite, who are literate, use English as a primary language and have access to the web and skill in presenting their message online, who are currently dominating Cyber Islamic Environments. This may mean that specific perspectives of interpretation associated with these groups, and even senses of 'mission', dominate when casual browsers look up 'Islam' using search-engines or surf the net for Islamic themes.

Other perspectives are also 'out there'. How many are found and read by those outside specific frameworks and circles of understanding? How will Cyber Islamic Environments change, when under-represented languages such as Urdu, Persian and Arabic start to emerge in greater depth online? What will the impact on Islam and Muslim understanding be, when areas with limited web access become further 'enfranchised', and the technological medium itself shifts to adopt further innovations and developments which transform the nature of the web and how it is utilized by users? These are subjects for future observation and research.

There is no single Cyber Islamic identity or community. The probability of one emerging, even if desired, becomes less and less likely as more perspectives emerge online. These perspectives may or may not choose to connect with each other, or accept the notions of 'authority' presented by those sites representing Islam on the web. They may or may not accept approaches to ritual, interpretation and sources, nor wish to be linked to a 'portal' claiming to represent the Muslim world online. They may or may not represent the 'success' of their perspective or their website by the number of hits or visitors to their site, or the number of times a search-engine places them at the top of the Internet 'hierarchy' for a particular subject. They may or may not care whether other Muslim perspectives agree with them or 'digitally' ostracize them.

Given these and other issues, and the unstructured nature of the web, observers and net users are faced with issues of how they personally approach the sites and the material contained on them. The net is changing on a daily basis. Millions of new sites emerged annually, a proportion of which contain Islam-related material. 'Old pages' and versions of perspectives may disappear, without being recorded or stored for posterity. How does one approach a constantly evolving and updating library of material about Islam and Muslims, whose shelves may 'change virtually' as soon as the reader enters the door?

In the past, a scholar of Islam may have learnt about Islamic law through a set pattern of education, utilizing texts that had remained unchanged for centuries. New opinions could only be accessed through travelling long distances to sit at the feet of scholars. Books may have been rare, and hand-copied. The descendants of these scholars, whilst utilizing similar sources, can now access many of them from their desktop computers. They can encounter the opinions and interpretations of others throughout the world, sharing perspectives and ideas, formulating approaches to knowledge. The more material that becomes available online, perhaps the more such scholars will experience information overload. They may also feel that their position is threatened when digital networks transcend traditional systems of knowledge and authority. Who needs scholars, when surfers can increasingly access the Islamic libraries and information resources of the world and make up their own minds on issues? That is one possible model. It needs to be recognized that whilst the information is 'out there', methodological approaches to its utilization still need to be taught. A central issue, therefore, is how material in Cyber Islamic Environments is managed, updated and accessed. The keys to knowledge are electronic. Will the web-designers in Cyber Islamic Environments in the future also be Islamic scholars, controlling the scope and presentation of information for the masses? Will computer skills be a central component in education received in Islamic educational contexts, including traditional schools of law and mosque schools? Again, these are patterns and interactions to be observed, analysed and recorded.

Even in a virtual world, not everything can be accomplished electronically. It may be possible to pray online, or approach authority, or even have a religious experience. Those promoting an electronic *umma* may stress the communality of the web. However, can this replace human action? Organizations or individuals in charge of Islamic websites may not deliberately set out to replace traditional networks of authority with cyberspace networks. However, with all the discussion on the fluidity of Muslim identity online, the constructs of authority, and the representation of Islam, the human element is often overlooked. Cyberspace may inform how those human elements interact, and change or challenge existing 'real' structures. It may present or create new opportunities or platforms for individuals and communities. As well as introducing 'new' concepts, the net may also bind disparate communities or platforms sharing common aims together under 'Islamic' banners.

The cliché about the web enhancing the freedom of expression of individuals and communities through providing accessible resources and information globally, needs to be challenged when examined in Cyber Islamic contexts. Whilst more regions of the world are coming online, and service providers are increasing the opportunities for access amongst those with the economic resources and inclination to go online, attempts are being made to control the nature of the web and the information contained on it. The success of these control measures is perhaps debatable, although paradoxically 'improvements' in technology may increase the opportunities for control in some contexts. Whether the increased development of web service provision in the Gulf States and Saudi Arabia will further open up the area for Islamist opposition groups operating online, or whether there are sufficient censorship controls in place, is open to question. The commercial considerations associated with enhancing these regions' Internet service provision, including reduced costs for consumers, may result in the rapid increase in the number of people accessing the diverse Cyber Islamic Environments online. The mechanisms that some regimes seek in order to censor elements of this access may not be technically viable, reliable or in place. Some Muslim contexts are already being presented with challenges to their authority online, which had previously been inaccessible to large sections of their population.

Other contexts, with Muslim majority populations, that have attempted to present their perspectives on the Internet have been challenged by political and other forces countering their presentation of the 'facts'. In late 1998, the Tunisian government attempted to present its human rights record on the Internet, and applied the 'amnesty' name in doing so. The human rights organization Amnesty International challenged this perspective, and presented its own 'site-within-a-site' to do so. This is perhaps a model for other platforms and interests in diverse contexts – including Islamists or religious authorities seeking to challenge the status quo as presented online. Representation of human rights in relation to Cyber Islamic Environments is an important issue for future research.

Conceivably, this challenge can be extended to the practice of 'hacking'. Whether this becomes more sophisticated or is prevented by the tightening of web technologies is open to question. The Muslim Hackers' Club (MHC) present themselves as an 'education' resource, providing data and technological advice:

> As Muslims we must be aware of what's available and learn to defend ourselves. We at MHC are not a wild bunch of kids (in fact some of us aren't kids at all!). MHC aims to educate on hacking and virus and related matters. We don't advocate anyone's going out and infiltrating and infecting or destroying an innocent party's computer systems with a malicious intent designed to clear out or steal valuable data or bring their system to a halt. MHC actually thinks that we as Muslims must be responsible and use the knowledge obtained for [our] own education.[1]

The extent to which this 'control' is exercised may be open to question, even if members of the club are not involved directly. Who is to say when it is appropriate to hack an alternative Muslim perspective, or a non-Muslim site such as SuraLikeIt?

A number of Islamic agendas may see it as entirely appropriate within an 'information war' to hack rivals, to introduce viruses into computers, to simulate 'crashes', or to disrupt systems at will. This can operate at many levels. The Indonesian government, representing a Muslim-majority country, attacked a 'Virtual East Timor' during 1999, disrupting its webpages and replacing them with alternative messages. A 'neutral' Internet service provider was temporarily forced to close as a result.[2] On the other hand, technologies to prevent hacking are also becoming more sophisticated, causing some activists to suggest that a 'golden era' of hacking is over.[3] Whether this is true or not, a number of governments have invested in technologies to prevent (or induce?) hacking activities. Deficiencies were highlighted by the 1999 'Melissa' e-mail virus, which resulted in an extensive FBI search for its creator.[4] The United States of America Defense Department has invested heavily in this area, having identified it as an issue of strategic vulnerability, pointing to the nature of information about itself available online and the potential avenues for hackers.[5] This may mean less information about strategic issues, and reduced avenues for hackers. Governments are clearly worried: 'What we're concerned about is in the future, nations will have that same capability to destroy each other's infrastructure, not by bombs, but by cyber attack.'[6]

However, in the past, the skills of such individuals and groups have often eclipsed those of governmental and other platforms. Given the strategic orientation of the United States Defense Department against specific activist Muslim platforms, it could be assumed that there is a fear of Muslim hackers drawing on commonly available information to disrupt computer systems in either military or civilian contexts.

This fear is also expressed by governments in many Muslim-majority countries, in relation to their being infiltrated or hacked by Islamist or other opposition parties.[7] This has led to caution in the development of web service provision by some, who are concerned about their inability to 'control' the Internet. They may have observed the ironic situation of Malaysian Prime

Minister Mahathir Mohamad, an advocate of information technology in Malaysia, who was unable to control the online pronouncements of reform-centred opposition platforms (including Muslim groups) during the 'Anwar crisis'.[8]

One result of such 'fears' may be increased filtering of *all* Islam- and Muslim-related sites, even those (in the majority) with no political agenda or association with those platforms deemed activist or dangerous. Filtering technology that prevents a user from accessing sites containing specific key words raises the issue discussed earlier, of what a browser receives when inputting the words 'Muslim girls' into a search-engine facility, just as those inputting 'Islam' may locate sites which are not deemed representative by others. Filtering technology may prevent access to *any* site related to Islam, the Qur'ān, Muslims and other key words. These could include 'innocent' Muslim sites providing information about religious practices, specific decision-making structures, or linking disparate communities. Such filters could also prevent access to news and information about Islam provided by the many news providers online.[9]

This technology raises broader censorship issues, and some interesting paradoxes in terms of Cyber Islamic Environments. Some Muslim platforms and services might endorse filtering and censorship when associated with other issues, for example those related to sexuality, but actively protest when it is related to Islam. Whether any censorship or regulation is appropriate, or indeed fully technically feasible, is an issue that cannot be dealt with here. However, to highlight this issue, it is worth considering a report from Cyber Rights and Cyber Liberties (UK), centring on filtering software. The report noted that the Electronic Privacy Information Centre (EPIC) in the United States conducted a survey of filtering software in relation to 'family-friendly' filters, comparing levels of filtering when specific software was utilized to search for sites. EPIC notes serious discrepancies in the software, meaning that 'innocent' sites were also filtered out:

> The Wisdom Fund . . . which promotes social justice and interfaith understanding by disseminating The Truth About Islam, and by providing concise statements of Islamic values, beliefs, news, commentary, and resources for concerned Muslims, citizens, and activists was for example blocked by I-Gear, a filtering software

> (I-Gear is used in many schools in the US, particularly in Virginia where its manufacturer, Unified Research Laboratories, is based) in a test conducted by Peacefire . . . SmartFilter, blocked such web sites as Understanding Islam and the Muslims . . . and Welcome to Saudi Arabia: The Land of Islam pages . . .[10]

There may be, for some, an irony in pages promoting Saudi Arabia themselves becoming victim to a filtering technology that many in authority there wish to promote for their own subjects.

These questions of control emerge in a medium through which anyone with access to the appropriate technology can 'publish' (even if their creativity might not be browsed or read!). Issues associated with how individual Muslims project themselves and present notions of Muslim identity need to be considered in future research. Will the Internet allow assertive, and perhaps anonymous, Muslim identities to extend further? How fluid will these notions of identity be, given that current technology allows individuals to take on several 'identities' simultaneously on webpages, and through other associated electronic media, such as e-mail and chat rooms?[11] An individual's community or family Muslim identity could differ considerably from an anonymous online construct. Such differences *may* also be seen in other contexts, although specific platforms and interests are unlikely to 'cloak' themselves in the same way.

In the decade leading up to the millennium, Cyber Islamic Environments have emerged, evolved and proliferated. Considerable further work in observation, analysis and discussion of aspects within these environments needs to be considered. At the beginning of the 1990s, one could probably talk about such sites and list them on a single sheet of A4 paper. Now that is impossible, and research needs to become more specialized, whilst being aware that there is an interconnectivity between many sites in terms of concepts, ideals and identities. There are notions of what it means to be Muslim online. Constructs of Islam can be approached and analysed. Perhaps there should also be consideration of how the 'unique' aspects of Cyber Islamic Environments will simply become part of the ordinary representation of Islam and Muslims, as a generation of Muslims with specific social and cultural parameters grows up with a familiarity with the web. Why should it be different from books, television programmes, radio broadcasts and other media seeking to represent Islam and Muslims?

The Internet theorist Nicholas Negroponte asserts that the digital revolution is over, and that the Internet has become an everyday technology and not something that is extraordinary or bizarre.[12] Whilst there are many communities and individuals, Muslim and non-Muslim, who are not 'wired', the phenomenon itself is well established in many contexts, and has become more affordable and accessible for many. The English-language monopoly has been broken, and other languages are increasingly applied to express Muslim opinions or concepts. There is nothing extraordinary about the existence of Muslim platforms and perspectives online. The Internet has opened new opportunities for communication. The methods in which that communication takes place may themselves now evolve further, contained within the broad parameters of information technology, and becoming further accepted as a means by which individual and group Muslim thought and expression can be presented to others.

Cyber Islamic Environments are in a transition period. Technological shifts will mean that other interfaces could be applied to access the web, such as digital telephones or televisions, perhaps circumnavigating controlled networks. The access speed to websites may also increase, although paradoxically the success of the web has slowed access as millions of new sites emerge on a regular basis. The desire to 'publish' online is unlikely to diminish, increasing the plethora of Islam-related sites. Tools to assist in selecting which material to read are likely to be popular, including guides and 'roadmaps'.

The distractions of the net (well known to all surfers) and the different ways through which texts can be accessed and read are likely to increase. How can an individual possibly obtain the information about Islam that she or he requires? Whereas several years ago the choice of Qur'ān translations was relatively small, now there are many different versions and formats. Basic information, for example, relating to the pillars of Islam, has in a way become less accessible, as the number of sites about each foundation of the religion increases daily. Obtaining a sense of direction for casual readers and surfers may become progressively more difficult. A considerable amount of material is repeated on different sites, and some readers may be unable to distinguish between different interpretations and constructs, many presenting themselves as definitive authorities. Individuals with the time and inclination to 'surf beneath the surface' may be few in numbers, encouraging those able to manipulate the system.

Methodologies of approaching hypertext are in their infancy compared with print media, and the random nature of the web presents issues of accessing information. Unlike checking a library index of relatively fixed data, it is possible to miss crucial sites in a fluid and ever-changing environment where the choice of material is linked to a multiplicity of factors 'outside the library'. Even in the great library of Al-Azhar University, a physical browser knows that the material on Islam and Muslim issues is probably going to be in the same place as on previous visits, and that the books themselves remain the same. It is said that an individual can never 'finish' reading the Qur'ān, because of the levels of understanding and complexities contained within it, as well as the text's esoteric qualities. The same could be said for certain online versions of the text, whose presentation and commentaries are constantly being updated to accommodate shifts in perspective and technological innovation, whilst the essential translation of the meaning may remain the same, and the Arabic text is universally constant.

Elements of participation in Cyber Islamic Environments may increase, enhancing the 'globalized' aspects of specific movements and platforms. The disconnected nature of interacting with text or pictures may shift. Why discuss issues through typing on screen in real time, when a camera mounted on the monitor will allow face-to-face interaction? Why send e-mail to an authority, when an individual can interact personally online with a 'real person'. These aspects may not be desirable in certain contexts, or indeed technically possible given that many Cyber Islamic Environments have hundreds or thousands of visitors a day. How will such interaction shift, and who will determine the 'Islamic' etiquette and boundaries?

There is no doubt that any Muslim platform that successfully approaches an educated élite and communicates with them on a regular basis will exert influence and power that transcends traditional networks. Those networks that disregard such developments, believing them inappropriate for their social and cultural context, may be unable to react to, or catch up with, the speed of technical progress. Given that technology is becoming cheaper and potentially easier to use, who is to say that small village mosques, even those without electricity, would not be influenced by the donation of a portable computer with satellite access, linked to a 'decision-making' network? As a tool for religious and political mobilization beyond conventional and/or state-controlled media, this could be effective and relatively inexpensive. Sermons could be heard and broadcast in real time and opinions on specific issues presented. It is feasible for this technology to empower and inform those who cannot progress through traditional channels, such as some women living in religious-cultural systems that may inhibit their freedom of movement or self-expression, including *purdah*. In practice, there may be issues of access to the appropriate equipment and networks. Those operating in minority contexts may also utilize Cyber Islamic Environments to express themselves.

Power struggles for the hearts, minds and souls of Muslims can now be enacted online. It may be only a small percentage of the billion-plus Muslims in the world who actually utilize the Internet. That percentage will increase, and so will the influence of certain parties operating in the medium. This is a formative period, and a great deal still has to be learnt by those operating in Cyber Islamic Environments (and observing them) about how the full potential of systems can be applied to suit specific agendas and purposes. The motivation cannot expected to be uniform, nor at times altruistic.

Much is done by Muslims in the name of Islam that is dismissed as inappropriate, or worse, by other Muslims. Not every surfer (Muslim or non-Muslim) is able to make appropriate judgements, or possess the knowledge to determine 'the truth'. Perhaps this is just part of a dialogue that transcends the Internet and its relatively short history. It is a wider philosophical and theological question that has been dominant throughout civilization. Earlier generations of scholars in Muslim and non-Muslim contexts would recognize the arguments, which have informed and shaped human history.

Whilst there is talk of new frontiers being transcended through the Internet, the human aspect is often subsumed by the technological one. Taking a step back, one can observe a longer process relating to how knowledge is transmitted and interpreted. Within specific Islamic networks, information operated on 'circuits' between authorities and scholars, whom the curious with the accessibility and economic power to do so visited to acquire knowledge. This information was stored, and transmitted to others through the same network. It was commentated on, and reinterpreted and presented in diverse languages and cultural contexts. It shared a common label, although notions of identity and conceptual frameworks differed in varied contexts. Reliance was placed by some on particular interpretations, whilst others remained in the 'minority' or were dismissed or even attacked. Notions of ritual and ultimate authority might be constant, with minor variations. Concepts associated with esoteric dimensions of interpretation remained on the fringes for some, and central to others.

With the Internet, networks of communication may have become quicker. Levels of interactivity have been enhanced, and notions of identity transformed for many. At the heart of the system, Islam contains elements that are shared, even as hundreds of new 'Islam' sites emerge monthly. This constancy is itself an important facet of Cyber Islamic Environments, a commonality that can be detected by Muslim and non-Muslim observers and surfers, even if it is not always recognized by site authors themselves. This is not to arrogate a predetermined identity, simply to recognize the shared symbols, ritual, sources and identities that coexist in Cyber Islamic Environments that are not necessarily mutually interactive or pacific. Is it necessary to distinguish between, for example, Ṣūfī sites and Wahhabi sites? On one level, perhaps, they are all 'Virtually Islamic'.

Whether Cyber Islamic Environments assist or detract in the quest for knowledge or the enhancement of Islam is a question for future discussion. The Qur'ān itself identifies the nature and complexities of knowledge, and how much is still 'unknown': 'Say: "If the ocean were ink (wherewith to write out) the words of my Lord sooner would the ocean be exhausted than would the words of my Lord even if we added another ocean like it for its aid."'[13]

The importance of acquiring and preserving knowledge about Islam is emphasized in several sources, and education is seen as a key element in the development of identity and community. The transmission of knowledge is interpreted as a duty, and special status attributed to transmitters. Differences in opinion within this knowledge can be acceptable, although there is evidence of conflict amongst Muḥammad's close companions relating to the recording of knowledge, even when he was on his deathbed.[14] The Qur'ān seeks that differences of opinion are brought to God, and to Muḥammad.[15] Certain differences are acceptable, on specific issues, perhaps relating to the meaning of words or the historical context of a verse, if not the overall impact or essence of meaning of verses. Dialogues associated with such differences have extended into cyberspace.

To conclude, Muslim individuals, platforms and communities may configure their identities in relation to the Internet, and inform themselves and others through Cyber Islamic Environments. As a key to understanding aspects of contemporary Islamic developments, the Internet is an important resource for rapidly updated information. As a system of knowledge provision and dissemination, it can erode certain traditional networks, but also has the potential to enhance or increase the power and influence of platforms and individuals. As an area for research, the subject is currently under-represented, and requires further in-depth study on specific aspects associated with Cyber Islamic Environments. Theories relating to levels of patronage, attitudes to representation, and concepts of identity and authority require analysis over a broad time frame, to accommodate technological and social developments and reactions to the Internet.

*Virtually Islamic* has been an attempt to provide an introductory snapshot of Cyber Islamic Environments. It is hoped that this will initiate dialogues and provide a platform for future work in this area. Muslim and Islamic developments in cyberspace should be seen as part of an evolutionary process, stretching back to the initial Revelation received by Muḥammad on Mount Ḥirā' in the year 610. Many of the dialogues and interactions contained on the web have precedents elsewhere in Islamic history.

At the time of writing, transformations of identity are taking place and concepts of knowledge evolving online. Whether these are more rapid in computer-mediated contexts than in other contexts is open to question. Such shifts are not unique to cyberspace, or to this period in history. In this book, it has been possible to note certain changes and transitions on the web in relation to Islam. However, to paraphrase the computer 'prophets', it has been said that a 'web year' is the equivalent of several years' real-time development. Whilst technological evolution may be compressed in terms of 'web years', humanity still operates in real time. It will only be through the distance of decades that the overall impact of the Internet can really be assessed, in order to establish whether Cyber Islamic Environments are *really* a significant turning-point in communication about Islam and Muslims.

# *Notes*

## Chapter 1: Introduction

[1] *Microsoft Flight Simulator 98*, CD-ROM (Microsoft Corporation, 1997).

[2] The term *Cyber* is taken from the Greek verb 'to pilot'. The origins of the term *Cyberspace* have been discussed extensively elsewhere. The term first emerged in William Gibson's science fiction novel *Neuromancer* (London: Gollancz, 1984).

[3] Examples of search-engines and directories include:

**Yahoo!**
*http://www.yahoo.com*
**Excite**
*http://www.excite.com*
**Altavista**
*http://altavista.digital.com*

[4] Akbar S. Ahmed and Hastings Donnan, 'Islam in the Age of Postmodernity', in idem (eds), *Islam, Globalization and Postmodernity* (London: Routledge, 1994), 17.

[5] The term *ijtihād* has several definitions, and is associated with the pragmatic interpretation of Islamic sources in the light of contemporary conditions. See G. R. Bunt, 'Decision-making and *Idjtihād* in Islamic Environments: A Comparative Study of Pakistan, Malaysia, Singapore, and the United Kingdom', University of Wales (Lampeter), Ph.D., 1996.

[6] Anis Ahmad, interview with writer, 30 April 1995. Da'wa Academy, International Islamic University, Islamabad, Pakistan.

[7] For an overview of the Internet prior to 1995, see Ed Krol, *The Whole Internet* (Sebastopol, California: O'Reilly & Associates, Inc., second edn, 1994), 13–17. For a guide to the Internet, see Angus J. Kennedy, *The Internet: The Rough Guide 1999* (London and New York: Rough Guides Ltd, 1998).

[8] Material was also analysed for the writer's personal university lecturing purposes, as the Internet lent itself to subject areas such as 'Islam in the Contemporary World' and 'Islam in the West'.

[9] This term is discussed in depth in Steven G. Jones (ed.), *Cybersociety: Computer-Mediated Communication and Community* (Thousand Oaks, California, London and New Delhi: Sage Publications, 1995).

[10] Marshall McLuhan, Transcript of lecture at Florida State University, 1970. **VideoMcLuhan:**
*http://www.videomcluhan.com/lectures.htm*

[11] James W. Carey, *Communication as Culture: Essays on Media and Society* (London: Unwin Hyman, 1989), 5.

[12] Brian D. Loader, *The Governance of Cyberspace* (Thousand Oaks, California, London and New Delhi: Sage Publications, 1997), 6.

[13] Lance Strate, Ronald Jacobson and Stephanie B. Gibson, 'Electronic Landscape: An Introduction to Communication and Cyberspace', in idem (eds), *Communication and Cyberspace: Social Interaction in an Electronic Environment* (Cresskill, New Jersey: Hampton Press Inc., 1996), 1.

[14] Similarly, there will not be a detailed discussion here on the availability (or the lack of it) of Arabic-language technology to compose HTML or write e-mails, which clearly has implications in the presentation and content of Islam-related Internet sites. New software is now emerging into the market (including free Arabic e-mail), and this is identified as an area for future research.

[15] Several of these perspectives are discussed in Annemarie Schimmel's phenomenology of Islam, which demonstrates the variance in symbols, sacred space, sacred time, sacred action, approaches to Islamic sources, and conceptions of God. See Annemarie Schimmel, *Deciphering the Signs of God: A Phenomenological Approach to Islam* (Edinburgh: Edinburgh University Press, 1994).

[16] Liaquat Ali Khan, 'Islam and the Web', featured on his **CyberMomin**
*http://www.geocities.com/Athens/Oracle/5118/IslamWeb.htm*

[17] Dale F. Eickelman and James Piscatori, *Muslim Politics* (New Jersey: Princeton University Press, 1996), 125.

[18] Many Internet browsers now come with a media-player incorporated into the software. The free version of the popular media-player ***RealPlayer*** can also be downloaded from the Internet.
**RealNetworks**
*http://www.real.com*

[19] Ananda Mitra, 'Virtual Commonality: Looking for India on the Internet', in Steven G. Jones, *Virtual Culture: Identity and Communication in Cybersociety* (Thousand Oaks: Sage Publications, 1997), 76.

[20] Howard Rheingold, *The Virtual Community: Finding Connection in a Computerized World* (London: Secker & Warburg, 1994).

[21] M. 'Afīfī al-'Akitī, Belfast Islamic Centre, response to writer's questionnaire, 5 June 1998.

[22] Hojjatoleslam Seyyed Ḥassan Khumaynī [Khomeini], speech during visit to Islamic Republic News Agency (IRNA), Tehran, 3 June 1998.
*http://www.irna.com/ertehal/visit.html*

[23] This process is unfinished according to Tehranian. See Majid Tehranian, 'Taming Modernity: Towards a New Paradigm', in Ali Mohammadi (ed.), *International Communication and Globalization: A Critical Introduction* (London, Thousand Oaks, California and New Delhi: Sage Publications, 1997), 120–1.

[24] David Holmes, 'Introduction', in idem (ed.), *Virtual Politics: Identity and Community in Cyberspace* (London, Thousand Oaks, California and New Delhi: Sage Publications, 1997), 3.

[25] Hamid Mowlana, *Global Communication in Transition: The End of Diversity* (London, Thousand Oaks, California and New Delhi: Sage Publications, 1996), 132.

[26] Ali Mohammadi, 'Introduction: A Critical Reader in International Communication and Globalization in a Postmodern World.' in idem, *International Communication*, 3.

[27] Tehranian, 'Taming Modernity', 157.

[28] Ninian Smart, *The World Religions* (Cambridge: Cambridge University Press, 1989), 9.

[29] Mowlana, *Global Communication*, 132.

[30] Huma Ahmad, 'Muslims on the Internet: The Good, the Bad . . . the Ugly'.

**Huma Ahmad**

*http://www.jannah.org/me/internet.html*

The term *MUD* is an acronym for 'Multi-User Dungeon', a term which now has wider implications than its original computer-games context, to suggest areas on the Internet where users are able to engage in real-time dialogues using electronic mail. A 'chatroom' performs a similar function on the Internet. The term *kuffar* (*sic*) is meant here in the context of 'non-believer' (of Islam), from the Arabic word *kufr*: non-belief.

ISNET – it is assumed that this refers to the Islamic Network chatroom which is primarily in Bahasa Indonesia (Indonesian). See
*http://www.isnet.org./archive-milis/archive99/may99/0817.htm*

[31] Rudolf Otto, *The Idea of the Holy: An Inquiry into the Non-rational Factor in the Idea of the Divine and its Relation to the Rational*, trans. John W. Harvey (London and New York: H. Milford; Oxford University Press, 1923).

[32] *Chambers Twentieth Century Dictionary*, ed. A. M. Macdonald (London: Chambers, 1977), 1399.

[33] Smart, *The World Religions*, 13.

[34] **Virtually Islamic**
*http://www.virtuallyislamic.com*

## Chapter 2: Primary forms of Islamic expression online

[1] The Qur'ān, *Sūrat al-'Alaq* or *'Iqrā* (The Clot or Read) [96], *The Qur'ān: Text, Translation and Commentary* ('Abdullāh Yūsuf 'Alī, Jeddah: Islamic Education Centre, 1934, 1946), 1761.

[2] This view is disputed by some Shī'a Muslims, who contend that 'Alī ibn Abī Ṭālib instigated the compilation of the Qur'ān. This has been highlighted on the Internet, in various sites, but it is not proposed to enter into this dispute here.
**Al-Islam**
*http://www.al-islam.org/encyclopedia/chapter8/4.html*

[3] The term *Suwar* is used for chapters within the Qur'ān: singularly known as *Sūra,* this is one of several terms which have effectively been turned into 'Islamic English', so that reference is often made to 'suras'. The term 'Islamic English' was first discussed by Ismā'īl Rājī al-Fārūqī, and issues surrounding transliteration were raised by Barbara Daly Metcalf. See Ismā'īl Rājī al-Fārūqī, *Towards Islamic English* (Virginia: International Institute of Islamic Thought, 1986); Barbara Daly Metcalf, *Making Muslim Space in North America and Europe* (Berkeley and London: University of California Press, 1996), xv–xix.

[4] The term *imām* can be applied in several different ways. Whilst it now can have the connotation in English of a mosque or community leader (the equivalent of a priest), in a general sense in Islamic Arabic *imām* usually refers to one who leads the prayers, not necessarily 'qualified' in the sense of trained clergy. In Shī'ā Islam, *Imām* has associations with religious leadership and continuity of spiritual authority, and for the purpose of clarity of discussion is capitalized.

[5] For an indication of the diversity of religious sources (including the Qur'ān) available via FTP in 1994 (prior to the mass application of the World Wide Web), see Krol, *The Whole Internet,* cited in chapter 1, note 7, 447–50.

[6] **Humanities Text Initiative, University of Michigan**
*http://www.hti.umich.edu*

[7] **The Koran**
*http://www.hti.umich.edu/relig/koran*
A printed version has been available in several editions and formats.

For example: *The Koran*, trans. M. H. Shakir (New York: Tahrike Tarsile Qur'an, Inc., fifth edn, 1988).

8 **Muslim Students Association of the University of Southern California** (MSA of USC)

*http://www.usc.edu/dept/MSA/quran/qmtintro.html*

9 This is available on the UK website About Islam and Muslims produced by the University of Northumbria's Islamic Society.

**About Islam and Muslims**

*http://www.unn.ac.uk/societies/islamic/*

10 Translation of *Sūrat al-Nahl* (The Bee) [16:90]. The printed version is Muḥammad Taqī-ud-Dīn Al-Hilālī and Muḥammad Muḥsin Khān, *Interpretation of the Meanings of the Noble Qur'ān in the English Language* (Riyadh: Maktba Dar-us-Salam Al Madīna Al-Munawwara, 1985 edn, reprinted 1993). The online version (cited in the quotation) is on the **About Islam and Muslims** website, ibid.

11 *Surat al-Nahl* 16:90, trans. Shakir.

**Humanities Text Initiative, University of Michgan**

*http://www.hti.umich.edu/bin/kor-idx?type=DIV0&byte=406637*

12 *Surat al-Naḥl* 16:90, trans. Marmaduke Pickthall, on Qur'ān comparative browser produced by Richard L. Goerwitz.

**Brown University Scholarly Technology Group**

*http://goon.stg.brown.edu/quran_browser/pqeasy.shtml*

13 Amongst the languages the writer has accessed Qur'ān translations are Chinese, French, German, Italian, Spanish, Turkish and Urdu.

French: **Le Saint Coran**

*http://www.orst.edu/groups/msa/quran/search_f.html*

Chinese: **Hong Kong Islamic Youth Organisation**

*http://www.glink.net.hk/~hkiya/c_quran.html*

German: **Der Heilige Koran**

*http://www.orst.edu/groups/msa/quran/index_g.html*

Italian: **Il Sacro Corano**

*http://www.geocities.com/Athens/Forum/8919/framec.htm*

Spanish: **El Sagrado Corán**

*http://www.orst.edu/groups/msa/quran/index_s.html*

Turkish: **Türkçe Kuran**

*http://www.bilginet.com/kuran/1kuran.html*

Swahili: **Qur'ani Tukufu**

*http://www.geocities.com/Athens/Parthenon/2355/*

Urdu: **The Mosque of the Internet**

*http://www.mosque.com*

14 Goerwitz, Qur'ān comparative browser.

15 No information as to the translation was provided.

**Muslim Students Association, University of Missouri-Rolla**

*http://www.uMr.edu/~msaumr/topics/*

[16] Dilip Hiro, *Islamic Fundamentalism* (London: Paladin Grafton Books, 1988), 122.

[17] **Radio al-Islam**

*http://www.islam.org/Radio/*

**Radio al-Islam** is not to be confused with Radio Islam, a Stockholm-based multilingual site that focuses on 'combating racism' (*sic*), which its author perceives as particularly prevalent amongst Israeli and Jewish people. It has been criticized for the content of its pages, which have hyperlinks to anti-Semitic and neo-Nazi webpages.

**Radio Islam**

*http://abbc.com/islam/english/english.htm*

This is discussed in Michael Whine, 'Islamist Organisations on the Internet', April 1998.

**The International Policy Institute for Counter-Terrorism**

*http://www.ict.org.il/articles/islamnet.htm*

[18] The twenty files that received the most requests (out of a top 100 listing) included at least ten of the 'radio' links, comprising 13.44 per cent of the total requests. The listing extends to fourteen pages of statistical analysis, and gives the overwhelming impression that the audio Qur'ān is the primary area of browser interest.

**Microsoft Usage Analyst** (6 October 1998)

*http://www.islam.org/Analysis/981026*

[19] Shaykh Abdul-Basit AbduSamat is also credited on a mirror-version of the site.

**Mosque of the Internet**

*http://www.mosque.com/recite.html*

[20] It is acknowledged here that download times are variable, and dependent on factors such as the surfer's location, connection and service provider location, as well as potential variable demands placed on similar elements relating to the webpage provider. The time of 'surfing' and the type of computer hardware and software utilized are also significant factors.

[21] This kind of interface would be a useful one for students: the writer's own students have utilized Radio Al-Islam in order to access the Qur'ān. It brings the text 'alive' to them, and offers one interpretation and explanation.

[22] 'Suratul Fatihah: Recitation by one of the brothers in Blacksburg'.

**Islamic Audio Studio (IAS), Islamic Centre of Blacksburg, Virginia**

*http://www.bev.net/community/sedki/icb_ra.html*

[23] IslamicBookstore.com also offers other products, and is one of a number of commercial enterprises selling Islamic goods online.

**IslamicBookstore.com**

*http://islamicbookstore.com/islamic_books/quranictarteel.shtml*

[24] One Arabic-language site (based in an American university) offers basic information, produced as scanned pages rather than HTML, making it difficult to browse.

**Tajweed**

*http://www.duke.edu/~maa3/Tajweed/Taj.html*

[25] **Answering Islam**

*http://answering-islam.org/Gilchrist*

[26] **Ahlul Bayt Digital Islamic Library Project (DILP)**

*http://www.al-islam.org/allah/index.html*

[27] Ahmad Ahmadi, Ayatullah Muhammad Hadi M'arifat, Baha al-Din Khorramshahi, Muhammad Husayn Ruhani, Abul Qasim Imami and 'Abbas Zaryab Khoi. 'The Geography of Qur'anic Accounts: Eight Questions from Six Scholars of the Qur'an', trans. from 'Geografiyaye Qisas-e Qur'an', published in *Bayyinat*, no. 3.

**Al Islam**

*http://www.al-islam.org/allah/index.html*

[28] **IslamicBookstore.com, 'Islamic Songs'**

*http://islamicbookstore.com/islamic_audios/islamic_songs.shtml*

[29] **DiWani**, 'Subahallah Alhamdullliah', *Jalan Yang Satu.*

*http://islamicbookstore.com/islamic_audios/islamic_songs.shtml*

[30] **Alan Godlas, Islamic Art, Music and Architecture**

*http://www.arches.uga.edu/~godlas/IslArt.html*

[31] **Mulids of Egypt**

*http://www.microstate.com/mm/mulid/*

January 1999

(link removed).

This site is discussed later in this book.

[32] **Cat Stevens**

*http://catstevens.com/*

[33] **Shī'a Muslim Salams, Marsiyas and Nohas**

*http://www.geocities.com/Athens/Agora/9220/*

[34] Ibid.

[35] As will be seen later in this book, some perspectives do not acknowledge the *aḥādīth* corpus as significant or binding. Others only follow elements within it.

[36] **US Muslim Students Association of the University of Southern California**

*http://www.usc.edu/dept/MSA/quran/qmtintro.html*

[37] Published as *Al-Maqasid*, trans. Noah Ha Mim Keller (no details were on the website regarding the publisher).

***Al-Maqasid*: Imam Nawawi's Manual on Islam**

*http://www.nbic.org/isru/Resources/Maqasid/*

[38] Al-Imaam Muhammad ibn Idris al-Shaafi'i, *Ar-Risaalah Fee Usool al-Fiqh*, trans. by M. Khadduri (Cambridge, Islamic Texts Society).

**Islamic Texts Society**
*http://www.islaam.com/articles/sunnah_shafi1.htm*

39 Ibn Rushd, *Bidayat al-Mujtahid wa Kifayat al-Muqtasid*, Belfast Islamic Centre.
**Ibn Rushd**
*http://ireland.iol.ie/~afifi/Ilm/Fiqh/BidayatMujtahid/Contents.htm*

40 For example, see: A. Zahoor and Z. Haq,
**Quotations from Famous Historians of Science**
*http://www.erols.com/zenithco/Intro11.html#refer1*

41 Philosophy in Cyberspace, Monash University (personal pages), Australia.
**Philosophy in Cyberspace**
*http://www-personal.monash.edu.au/~dey/phil/section1.htm)*

42 **Contemporary Legal Rulings in Shī'a Law in accordance with the rulings (*fatāwā*) of Ayatullāh al-'Uzma al-Sayyid 'Ali al-Husayni al-Seestani**
*http://www.al-islam.org/laws/contemporary/index.html*

43 *Sūrat al-Mu'minūm* [23:52–3], trans. 'Abdullāh Yūsuf 'Alī, *The Alim*, CD-Rom (USA: ISL Software Corporation, n.d.).

## Chapter 3: Muslim diversity online

1 Aziz al-Azmeh, *Islam and Modernities* (London and New York: Verso, 1993), 89.

2 Dale F. Eickelman and James Piscatori, *Muslim Politics* (Princeton: Princeton University Press, 1996), 20–1, citing Clive S. Kessler, 'New Directions in the Study of Islam: Remarks on Some Trends and Prospects', *Jurnal Antropologi Dan Sosiologi* 18 (1990), 3–22, 15.

3 **Yahoo! search-engine**
*http://search.yahoo.co.uk*
21 November 1998

4 **Lycos City Guide: Makkah**
*http://cityguide.lycos.com/middle_east/arabian_peninsula/SAUMakkah.html*

5 **Islamic Affairs Department, Royal Embassy of Saudi Arabia**
*http://www.iad.org/*

6 M. 'Afifī al-'Akitī, Belfast Islamic Centre, response to writer's questionnaire, 5 June 1998,

7 Ibid.

8 Ibid.

9 Abdal Hakim Murad, 'British and Muslim?'
**Belfast Islamic Centre**
*http://ireland.iol.ie/~afifi/Articles/british.htm*

[10] **Muslims Online**
*http://www.muslimsonline.com/*

[11] Ibid.

[12] Ibid.

[13] **Idara Dawat-O-Irshad, USA Inc**
*http://irshad.org/idara/home.htm*

[14] **Islamic Gateway**
*http://www.ummah.net/aboutig.html*

[15] Ibid.

[16] **Sufi Fighting Arts Movie Production**
*http://www.ummah.net/fighting/movie.htm*
14 December 1998.

[17] Islamic Gateway.

[18] *Islamic Gateway*, CD-ROM, version 2.6 (London, 1998).

[19] Nikki Keddie, *Roots of Revolution* (New Haven: Yale University Press, 1991), 7 (quotation not attributed).

[20] **World Association of Muslim Youth (WAMY)**
*http://www.wamy.org/*

[21] **Al-Islam**
*http://www.al-islam.org/gallery/sound3.htm#Allah*

[22] **ArabNet**
*http://www.arab.net/links/yn/welcome.html*

[23] **Shia Ismaili Web**
*http://www.hal-pc.org/~amana/ismaili.html*

[24] **The Sun's House**
*http://www.irna.com/occasion/ertehal/index-e.htm*

[25] **Image of Sunshine**
*http://www.irna.com/ertehal/images/family-e.htm*

[26] See John Simpson and Tira Shubart, *Lifting the Veil: Life in Revolutionary Iran* (London: Hodder & Stoughton, 1995).

[27] This site requires a Farsi font browser, available on the index page.
**IRNA**
*http://www.irna.com/ertehal/rahbar/index.htm*

[28] This report discussed the views of Āyatullāh Aḥmad Jannati, who criticized the Internet during Friday prayers in Tehran. 'Iranian Conservative Slams Internet', BBC News, BBC Online Network, 23 January 1999
*http://news2.thdo.bbc.co.uk/hi/english/world/middle%5Feast/newsid%5F261000/261300.stm*

[29] 'Ayatollah Khomeini on the Web', BBC News, BBC Online Network, 2 June 1998
*http://news2.thdo.bbc.co.uk/hi/english/world/middle%5Feast/newsid%5F104000/104312.stm*

'Late-imam-works-internet', IRNA Iranian News Agency, 2 June 1998

*http://www.irna.com/newshtm/eng/11163523.htm*
(link deleted)

[30] **Islamic Centre of England (London)**
*http://www.ic-el.org/*

[31] Ibid., December 1998 calculation.

[32] **United Muslims of America**
*http://fortyhadith.khomeini.com/*

[33] **Qabas**
*http://www.qabas.net*

[34] ***Ma'rifat***
*http://www.qabas.net/marifat/*

[35] *The Christian Science Monitor*: Scott Peterson, 'Iran's Newest Revolution: Holy Texts Go On Computer', 13 October 1998.
**CyberUrbanity List Archive**
*http://www.csmonitor.com/*

[36] **Islam-Iran**
*http://www.islam-iran.org/foundations/link17.htm*

[37] **The Constitutionalists Movement of Iran**
*http://www.irancmi.org/index3.htm*

[38] Keddie, *Roots of Revolution*, 217.

[39] **The Official Ali Shariati Site**
*http://www.shariati.com*

[40] Bahrain is ruled by a Sunnī minority, and one of the principal opposition groups is the Islamic Front for the Liberation of Bahrain, whose leader is Shaykh Abdel Amīr al-Jamrī. However, at the time of writing, there were no obvious Shī'a websites associated with this organization. Several perspectives associated with Shī'a beliefs in Lebanon can be located, and are discussed later in this book.

[41] Estimated at 60–5 per cent of the 97 per cent Muslim population. The total population of Iraq is estimated at 22,219,289 (July 1997 est.), according to the *CIA World Factbook*.
**CIA World Factbook**
*http://www.odci.gov/cia/publications/factbook/iz.html*

[42] **Al-Islam**
*http://www.al-islam.org/biographies/khoei.htm*

[43] **Al-Khoei Foundation**
*http://www.al-khoei.org/updates.htm*

[44] **Iman Ali Foundation**
*www.seestani.org*

[45] **Khoja Shī'a Ithnā 'Asharī World Federation**
*http://www.world-federation.org*

[46] Ibid.
*http://www.world-federation.org/wf_newsofdeath.htm*
12 December 1998.

[47] Amir G. N. Lakha, 'Why The Need For A Jiba Web Site?'
**JIBA Europe**
*http://www.jiba.org/*

[48] 'HIV and AIDS make their presence felt in the community', *Samachar*, 31, 1.
**The Federation of Khoja Shī'a Ithnā 'Asharī Jamaats of Africa**
*http://www.africafederation.org/fedsamachar/sep98_index.htm*

[49] Bunt, 'Decision-making', 218–19 and *passim.*

[50] **The Chishti Habibi Soofie Islamic Order**
*http://www.soofie.org.za/html/pseudo_sufism.html*

[51] Ibid.
*http://www.soofie.org.za/*

[52] **Naqshbandi Sufi Way**
*http://www.naqshbandi.org/frmabout.htm*

[53] Shaykh Muḥammad Hisham Kabbani, 'History and Guidebook of the Saints of the Golden Chain'
*http://www.naqshbandi.net/haqqani/sufi/NaqshSufiWay/Sh_Nazim.html*

[54] **Dhikr in Congregation** (*Khatm-ul-Khwajagan*)
*http://www.naqshbandi.org/frmpract.htm*

[55] The term *mawlid* can also refer to the celebration of saints' birthdays, and was featured in a site presenting photographic and sound records of rituals, in the context of Egypt. The hyperlink became 'broken' by the time of publication. In addition to the *Virtually Islamic* website, readers may wish to check the site's former url for any updates:
**Mulids of Egypt**
*http://www.microstate.com/mm/mulid/*

[56] **The Royal Malaysian Naqshbandi Group**, 'Praising the Prophet: The Mawlid'
*http://www.naqshbandi.org/frmpract.htm*

[57] **The Doctrine of Ahl Al-Sunna versus the 'Salafi' Movement**
*http://www.naqshbandi.org/ottomans/wahhabis.htm*

[58] **Attasia Ṭarīkah**
*http://www.attasia.org*

[59] **Quraan and Islamic Sciences City**
*http://members.tripod.com/Flowersun/home.html*

[60] Comments from visitors. Typographical errors corrected.
**Chisti Qadhiri**
*http://www.geocities.com/Athens/Olympus/5352/geobook.html*

[61] **Dar ul-Iman**
*http://www.chishti.com/corder/posture_5.htm*
February 1999
This link is no longer available. The webmaster advised me in April 1999 that the site was 'in hiatus', with no plans for a relaunch. In addition to the *Virtually Islamic* website, readers may wish to check the site's main pages for any updates:
*http://www.chisti.com*

[62] Ibid., 'The Universe of the Breath', February 1999
*http://www.chishti.com/corder/universe_of_the_breath.htm*
(link deleted, see previous note).

[63] Ibid., 'Sufi Healing', February 1999
*http://www.chishti.com/corder/about_sufi_healing.htm*
(link deleted).

[64] Such attribution of the physical benefits of prayer have some precedent within Muslim medical texts, from Sunnī and other perspectives.

[65] **Tijāniyya Tariqat**
*http://www.geocities.com/Athens/9189/shhassan.html*

[66] **Ṣūfism in Indonesia**
*http://www.geocities.com/Athens/5738/frame.htm*

[67] **Ṣūfi Order of the West**
*http://www.sufiorder.org/indexie.html*

## Chapter 4: Politics, Islam and the Net

[1] For a history of the Taliban, see Peter Marsden, *The Taliban: War, Religion and the New Order in Afghanistan* (Karachi, Lahore and Islamabad: Oxford University Press; London and New York: Zed Books, 1998).

[2] *Dharb-i-M'umin*: 25/07/1419 (Hijri), 15 November 1998.
**Taliban Online**
*http://www.ummah.net/dharb*

[3] Ibid.

[4] Ibid.

[5] **Taleban Islamic Movement of Afghanistan**
*http://www.taleban.com*

[6] Jamiat-e-Islami Afghanistan is not necessarily connected with other organizations with the same or similar names located elsewhere.
**Jamiat-e-Islami Afghanistan**
*http://www.jamiat.com/goals/goal.html*

[7] Ibid.

[8] 'A Short Biography of the Martyred Leader, Abdul Ali Mazari (R.A.)'.
**Hazera Press/Hezb-e Wahdat**
*http://www.hazara.com*

[9] 'The Plight of the Afghan Woman'.
**Afghanistan Online**
*http://www.afghan-web.com/woman/*

[10] Ibid.

[11] 'Women in Islam'.
**Afghanistan Online**
*http://www.afghan-web.com/woman/muslima.html*

[12] A. Raffaele Ciriello, 'Photographs of Afghan Women'.
**Afghanistan Online**
*http://www.afghan-web.com/ciriello/woman/*

[13] **Revolutionary Association of the Women of Afghanistan (RAWA)**
*http://www.rawa.org/*

[14] Ibid.

[15] **Islamic Republic of Pakistan**
*http://www.pak.gov.pk/*

[16] **Pakistan People's Party**
*http://www.ppp.org.pk/*

[17] **Pakistan Tehreek-e-Insaf**
*http://www.insaf.com/tehreek_home.html*

[18] **Jamā'at i Islāmī Pakistan**
*http://www.jamaat.org*

[19] Ibid. 'Jamaat poised for ouster of Nawaz government',
14 November 1998.
**Jamā'at i Islāmī Pakistan**
*http://www.jamaat.org/news/newsarchive98/pr111498.html*

[20] Ibid. 'Saying Merry Christmas to Christians'
16 December 1998
*http://www.jamaat.org/ (deleted article)*

[21] Ibid.

[22] Ibid. 'JI moot adopts charter for women'
*http://www.jamaat.org/news/newsarchive98/pr102498.html*

[23] Ibid. 'What is wrong with Motorway?'
16 December 1998
*http://www.jamaat.org/ (deleted article)*

[24] **Muttahida Quami Movement (MQM)**
*http://www.mqm.org*

[25] **Tanzeem-e-Islami Pakistan**
*http://www.tanzeem.org.pk*

[26] See Bunt, 'Decision-making', 44–5.

[27] **Tanzeem-e-Islami Pakistan**
*http://www.tanzeem.org.pk/news/news.htm*
14 December 1998.
These webpages did not contain an archive at the time of writing, and this story had been removed from the site. Similar statements can be located through the above hyperlink.

[28] Ibid.
*http://www.tanzeem.org.pk/ameer/ameer.htm*

[29] **Jammu Kashmir Liberation Front (JKLF)**
*http://www.geocities.com/CapitolHill/Lobby/8125/fpage.html*

[30] **BBC Online Network,** 'Indian army Website ambushed', 16 October 1998
*http://news2.thdo.bbc.co.uk/hi/english/world/south%5Fasia/newsid%5F194000/194844.stm*

[31] Anwar Ibrahim was jailed for six years on 14 April 1999, with the potential for a further sentence on other charges.

[32] **ADIL Answers,** 'Five Supreme Ironies', 26 January 1999
*http://members.easyspace.com/reformasi/answer2.htm*

[33] **Prime Minister's Office of Malaysia**
*http://www.smpke.jpm.my/*

[34] **Department of Islamic Development of Malaysia, Prime Minister's Department,**
**Ruangan Soal Jawab Agama bersama Jabatan Kemajuan Islam Malaysia (JAKIM).**
*http://www.islam.gov.my/*

[35] Ibid.
*http://www.islam.gov.my/soal/soal.htm*

[36] Ibid., 'Deviationist Teachings in Malaysia'
*http://www.islam.gov.my/*

[37] Ibid.

[38] **Reuters Press Agency**, 'Malaysian Technological Sufis Await Islam Messiah', 13 July 1994. The *Dar al-Arqam* title is utilized elsewhere, by diverse organizations with very different perspectives (and no connection with) the Malaysian platform. For example, see
**The Muslim Converts' Association of Singapore**
**Darul Arqam Singapore**
*http://www.darul-arqam.org.sg/*

[39] For Mahathir's speeches, see 'Prime Minister on Malaysia'.
**Institut Kefahaman Islam Malaysia (IKIM)**
*http://www.ikim.gov.my/s301–7.htm*

[40] For example, see
**UMNO Youth Movement**
*http://www.umnoyouth.org.my*

[41] **Parti Islam SeMalaysia (PAS)**
*http://www.jaring.my/pas*

[42] **PAS Johore**
*http://www.geocities.com/CapitolHill/Senate/5059/a_rasmi.htm*

[43] Bunt, 'Decision-making', ch.3.

[44] Anwar Ibrahim, 'The Asian Renaissance' (n.d.), download from
**Anwar Ibrahim and Gerakan Reformasi Malaysia**
*http://reformasi.cjb.net*

[45] **Anwar Ibrahim**
*http://anwaribrahim1.com/*

[46] **Laman Reformasi**
*http://members.tripod.com/~mahazalim/*

[47] **The Reformation Movement Starts Here!**
*http://www.cyberway.com.sg/~nassir/*

[48] **Webpress Alternative**
*http://www.webpres.com.my/malaysia*

[49] **A Card for Anwar Ibrahim**
*http://cardforanwar.hypermart.net*

[50] **ABIM (Angkatan Belia Islam Malaysia) Online**
*http://www.jaring.my/abim/english/index.html*

[51] **Majlis Ugama Islam Singapura**
*http://www.muis.gov.sg/*

[52] Inter Press Service, 'Sudan-Internet: Muslim Sect Sees "Moral Pollution" on Internet', 16 March 1998.

[53] Ibid.

[54] SilkiNet chairman Fouad Yashar, cited in **BBC News Online,** 'Surfing in the desert', 6 May 1998
*http://news2.thdo.bbc.co.uk/hi/english/sci/tech/newsid%5F88000/88821.stm*

[55] Reuters, 'Saudi Arabia Launches Internet', 25 January 1999.

[56] **King Faisal Foundation**
*http://www.kff.com*

[57] **Campaign for Democracy and Legal Rights (CDLR)**
*http://www.ummah.org.uk/cdlr/*

[58] Ibid.
*http://www.ummah.org.uk/cdlr/abouteng.html*

[59] Movement for Islamic Reform in Arabia (MIRA), 'Dispatches from Behind the Veil'.
**MIRA**
*http://www.miraserve.com/arabia/a5h2.htm*

[60] Al-Saūd House, Committee against Corruption in Saudi Arabia. (CACSA), 'Our Mission'.
**CASCA**
*http://www.saudhouse.com*

[61] Ibid.

*http://www.saudhouse.com/frontmen.htm*

[62] Ibid.

*http://www.saudhouse.com/abdul.htm*

[63] See the work undertaken on the following site:

**Arab Information Project at Georgetown University**

*http://www.georgetown.edu/research/arabtech*

[64] For example, see

**The Complete Guide to Palestine's Websites**

*http://www.birzeit.edu/links*

**Zipple**

*http://www.zipple.com/*

[65] **Hamas**

*http://www.hamas.org*

[66] Ibid.

*http://www.hamas.org/aff.htm*

*http://www.hamas.org/note.htm*

[67] **Palestine Information Centre**

*http://www.palestine-info.org*

[68] **Islamic Association of Palestine**

*http://www.iap.org*

[69] **Hezbollah**

*http://www.hezbollah.org/note.htm*

[70] **Hizbollah Central Press Office**

*http://www.hizbollah.org/hizb/definiti.html*

[71] **Hizbollah Central Press Office**

*http://www.hizbollah.org/hizb/picc.html*

[72] **Islamic Resistance Support Organization**

*http://www.moqawama.org/page2/f_vresis.htm*

[73] Ibid.

*http://www.moqawama.org/page2/f_vresis.htm*

[74] Ibid.

[75] Ibid.

*http://www.moqawama.org/martyrs/body.htm*

[76] **Al Kassam Shuhada Memorial**

*http://www.demon.co.uk/alquds/islamic.htm*

[77] Ibid., 'History of Al-Kassam'

*http://www.demon.co.uk/alquds/kataib.htm*

[78] Michael Whine, 'Islamist Organisations on the Internet', April 1998.

**The International Policy Institute for Counter-Terrorism**

*http://www.ict.org.il/articles/articledet.cfm?articleid=31*

[79] **Front Islamique du Salut**

*http://www.fisalgeria.org*

[80] **Bosnia-Net**
*http://www.fama.com*

[81] **Bosnet**
*http://www.bosnet.org/*

[82] **Bosanski Webring**
*http://www.webring.org/cgi-bin/webring?ring=bosnjaci;index*

[83] **Ḥizb ut-Ṭahrīr**
*http://www.hizb-ut-tahrir.com*

[84] The term *Al-Muhājiroun* is associated with Muḥammad's own close followers during his lifetime, and means 'the emigrants'. The original *muhājirūn* left Mecca with the Prophet at a time of persecution, to live in Medina. The event (in 622 CE) marked the first year of the Islamic calendar.

[85] 'The Policy of Al-Muhajiroun in The West'.
**Al-Muhājiroun**
*www.almuhajiroun.com*

[86] Ibid., 'Muslims will hound Blair wherever he goes!' *As Sahwa* 2:14 (January 1999). 'British Government's New laws to stop Islamic Activity!' *As Sahwa* 2:13 (December 1998)
*http://www.almuhajiroun.com*

[87] The Shari'ah Court of the UK, 'Fatwa or Divine Decree concerning Salman Rushdie'.
*As Sahwa* 2:11(October 1998). This 'fatwa' in itself could potentially be interpreted as incitement. This link was formerly on the original Al-Muhājiroun website, hosted by the Islamic Gateway, but the contents were transferred to a new web-address in 1999.
*http://www.almuhajiroun.com*

[88] **Omar Bakri Muḥammad OBM Home Page**
*http://www.obm.clara.net/*

## Chapter 5: Digital *minbar*: Islamic obligations and authority online

[1] This is based on the Online Islamic Propagation Team publication 'Salah: The Muslim Prayer' (n.d.).
**Online Islamic Propagation Team**
*http://members.aol.com/Palestine5*

[2] **CyberSalat**
*http://www.ummah.net/software/cyber*

[3] Ibid.

[4] Monzur Aḥmed, 5 December 1998, e-mail response to writer's questions.

[5] Fasting times are provided by:

**Ramadhan**

*http://www.ramadhan.org*

[6] The interface of the site allows for a full question (rather than just keywords) to be entered. This site also links into other search-engines.

**Ask Jeeves**

*http://www.askjeeves.com*

[7] This was a reproduction of a publication, and appeared on a University of Houston Muslim Students' Association page. Halal Foundation, *A Guide to Halal Food Selection, Illinois* (Islamic Food and Nutrition Council of America, n.d.).

**University of Houston Muslim Students' Association**

*http://www.uh.edu/campus/msa/articles/halal.html*

[8] **Islamic Finder**

*http://www.islamicfinder.org/finder*

[9] **Muslims Online**

*http://mailhost.muslimsearch.com/cgi-bin/search/muslim.cgi*

[10] The Arabic html was not 'browsable' at the time of writing, in the sense of being able to select key words or topics; the material is from scanned Arabic pages, and does not require an Arabic browser.

**Al-Moukhtar**

*http://www.al-mokhtar.com.lb/friday.htm*

[11] E-mail to writer from Ossama M. Khayat, Tawhid Islamic Movement in Lebanon, 15 June 1998.

[12] Ibid.

[13] This site scored approximately 15,000 visitors between January 1997 and June 1998.

**Aḥmed Deedat: Hear His Voice**

*http://home2.swipnet.se/~w–20479/Audio.htm*

[14] Aḥmed Deedat, 'His Holiness Plays Hide and Seek with Muslims'

*http://home2.swipnet.se/~w–20479/Hide.htm*

[15] **Yūsuf Qarādawī**

*http://www.qaradawi.net*

[16] **'Unofficial' Al-Azhar Page**

*http://www.ims.uwindsor.ca/~azhar*

[17] **Al-Azhar**

*http://www.alazhar.org*

[18] Mustafa Rawji, co-administrator, 'Aalim Network, e-mail response to writer's questions, 10 August 1998. Ahlul Bayt 'Aalim Network also organize the Al-Islam website, discussed in the survey on Shī'ia Islam in chapter 3.

[19] Ahlul Bayt 'Aalim Network. Search undertaken by writer on 2 June 1998.

[20] Selected topics from the 'Aalim Network e-mail listing during 1998. Square brackets contain this writer's brief definitions of technical terms. Ellipse brackets contain summary of decision. (Sender:
*owner-abdg-a@lists.Stanford.EDU*)

[21] E-mail: 'Aalim Network, Wearing Gold/Najasat of Dogs, 14 June 1998. (Sender:
*owner-abdg-a@lists.Stanford.EDU*)

[22] **The Islamic Assembly of North America (IANA) Fatwa and Research Centre**
*http://www.iana.org/*

[23] **Ask the Imam**
*http://islam.org/islamicity/dialogue/a1.htm*

[24] Ibid.
*http://islam.org:81/Imam/about.htm*
January 1999 (link deleted)

[25] Ibid., question 3578.

[26] Bunt, 'Decision-making', ch. 4.

[27] **Ask the Imam**, question 3921 (some typographical corrections).

[28] Ibid., question 2633 (some typographical corrections).

[29] **Queer Jihad**
*http://www.geocities.com/WestHollywood/Heights/8977/index.htm*

[30] **Queer Muslims**
*http://www.angelfire.com/ca2/queermuslims*

[31] **IslamiCity**
*http://209.141.1.6/dialogue/topics.htm*

[32] Ibid., 'Our Dialogue', question 343
*http://islamicity.org/islamicity/dialogue/q343.htm*

[33] Ibid., question 269
*http://islamicity.org/islamicity/dialogue/q269.htm*

[34] **Belfast Islamic Centre**
*http://ireland.iol.ie/~afifi/Articles/articles.htm*

[35] Ibid.
**Shaykh Dr ad-Darsh column**,
16 August 1996.
*http://ireland.iol.ie/~afifi/Ad-Darsh/16.8.96.htm*

[36] Ibid., 14 March 1997
*http://ireland.iol.ie/~afifi/Ad-Darsh/14.3.97.htm*

[37] **Baltimore Muslims**
*http://www.angelfire.com/ak/BaltoMuslims/advicefornew.html*

[38] **Answering Christianity**
*http://www.angelfire.com/ak/BaltoMuslims/answers.html*

[39] Ibid. (typographical errors edited by this writer).

[40] **The Answer to Answering Islam**
*http://www.submission.org/answering-islam-org.htm*

41 **Answering Islam**
*http://answering-islam.org.uk*
*http://answering-islam.org* (USA mirror site)

42 **Answering Islam**
*http://answering-islam.org.uk/policy.html*

43 In a perhaps extreme example, this writer sought information on Islam and China, and emerged on the Christian World Evangelisation Research Centre. See Gary R. Bunt, 'Islam in Cyberspace: Islamic Studies' Resources on the Internet', *Muslim World Book Review*, 18, 1, 5–6 (1997).

44 The Qur'ān, Sūra Al Baqara, 2:23, trans. Yūsuf Ali, *The Alim*, CD-ROM.

45 The Qur'ān, Sūra Al-Isrā', 17:88, trans. Yūsuf Ali, *The Alim*, CD-ROM.

46 SuraLikeIt, *Al-Muslimoon*, originally on the SuraLikeIt pages. Transliterations follow the SuraLikeIt format.
**SuraLikeIt**
*http://www.aol.com/SuraLikeIt*
disconnected at the time of writing
**SuraLikeIt UK**
*http://dspace.dial.pipex.com/suralikeit/*

47 SuraLikeIt.

48 SuraLikeIt, '*Al-Wasya*' (The Commandments), 1:15.

49 Reuters News Agency, 24 June 1998.

50 **Al-Azhar**
*http://www.alazhar.org*

51 AOL spokesperson, cited in Reuters report, 24 June 1998.

52 Mohamed Rayes, e-mail contribution to 'soc.religion.islam' discussion group, 23 June 1998, some typographical corrections.

53 **Masjid Tucson United Submitters International,**
'Challenging the Qur'an. What Went Wrong!'
*http://www.submission.org/challenge.html*

54 Ibid. The mathematics are derived from a number of sources linked into the site, under the title 'Mathematical Miracle of the Quran'.

55 **IslamFirst**
*http://www.angelfire.com/al/islamfirst*

56 The writer located SuraLikeIt using the Webcrawler search-engine.
**Webcrawler**
*http://www.webcrawler.com*

57 **SuraLikeIt UK**
*http://dspace.dial.pipex.com/suralikeit/*

58 The Muslim Hackers' Homepage is one example where such activity might be initiated, as it provides information and codes for entering

into specific computer systems, together with viruses to corrupt computers. The site was hosted by the Islamic Gateway (q.v.), which emphatically denied responsibility for content.

**Muslim Hackers' Homepage**

*http://www.ummah.net/mhc*

59 The Qur'ān, Surah Al-Muminun 23:52–3, trans. Yūsuf Ali, *The Alim* CD-ROM.

## Chapter 6: Cyber Islamic Futures

1 Muslim Hackers' Club (MHC), message posted on BIC News, 15 July 1998. MHC also has its own website.

**BIC News**

*http://ireland.iol.ie/~afifi*

**Muslim Hackers' Club**

*http://www.ummah.net/mhc*

2 Chris Nuttall, 'Virtual country "nuked" on Net', BBC News, 26 January 1999

**BBC News**

*http://news2.thdo.bbc.co.uk/hi/english/sci/tech/newsid%5F263000/ 263169.stm*

3 Gibby Zobel, 'A New Kind of Revolution', *The Big Issue*, 11–17 January 1999.

4 The alleged Melissa virus author, David Smith, a computer programmer from New Jersey, was arrested in April 1999. The FBI's National Infrastructure Protection Center, a special division created to track down computer-related crime, was credited with locating Smith.

5 Paul Stone, 'Internet Presents Web of Security Issues', September 1998.

**American Forces Press Service, American Forces Information Service**

*http://www.defenselink.mil/news*

6 Richard Clarke, US presidential co-ordinator for counter-terrorism, cited in 'US Cyber Terrorism Plea', BBC News, 22 January 1999.

*http://news2.thdo.bbc.co.uk/hi/english/world/americas/ newsid%5F260000/260855.stm*

7 Andrew Rathmell, 'Netwar in the Gulf', 9 January 1997. 'Netwar in the Gulf', *Jane's Intelligence Review* (January 1997), 29–32.

8 Chandra Muzaffar, 'ADIL Answers Five Supreme Ironies', 26 January 1999.

**ADIL**

*http://members.easyspace.com/reformasi/answer2.htm*

[9] This subject was discussed in Bunt, 'Islam in Cyberspace'.

[10] Yaman Akdeniz, 'What is wrong with Internet Rating Systems and Filtering Software', *The Chronicle* (June 1998).

**The Chronicle**

*http://www.thechronicle.demon.co.uk/archive/filter.htm*

[11] For a discussion on these constructs, see the article by Daniel Chandler, 'Personal Home Pages', 18 August 1998.

**Daniel Chandler**

*http://www.aber.ac.uk/~dgc/webident.html*

[12] Nicholas Negroponte, 'Beyond Digital', *Wired* 6.12 (December 1998).

**Wired**

*http://nicholas.www.media.mit.edu/people/nicholas/Wired/WIRED6–12.html*

[13] *Sūrat Al-Kahf* 'The Cave', 18:109, trans. Yūsuf Ali, *The Alim*, CD-ROM.

[14] See, for example, Sahih Al-Bukhari Hadith 1:114, narrated by Ubaidullah bin Abdullah, ibid.

[15] *Sūrat al-Nisā'* (The Women), 4:59, ibid.

# *Bibliography*

All transliterations of terminology and proper names follow their users' own systems. All URLs were correct at the time of going to press. Subsequent alterations are located on the *Virtually Islamic* website, together with a jump page to all listed sites. (*www.virtuallyislamic.com*)

## The Qur'ān: printed sources

A number of these printed sources are also located within Internet Sources.


'Alī, 'Abdullāh Yūsuf. *The Qur'an: Text, Translation and Commentary* (Jeddah: Islamic Education Centre, 1934, 1946).

Al-Hilālī, Muḥammad Taqī-ud-Dīn, and Muḥammad Muḥsin Khān. *'Interpretation of the Meanings of the Noble Qur'an in the English Language'* (Riyadh: Maktba Dar-us-Salam Al Madīna Al-Munawwara).

Pickthall, Marmaduke. *The Meaning of the Glorious Koran: An Explanatory Translation by Marmaduke Pickthall* (New York: Knopf, 1930).

Shakir, M. H. (trans.). *The Koran* (New York: Tahrike Tarsile Qur'an, Inc., fifth edn, 1988).


## The Qur'ān: Internet sources

Note: Some of the other websites listed later within this Bibliography also contain links to Qur'ān material. See Notes for full details.


**Der Heilige Koran**

*http://www.orst.edu/groups/msa/quran/index_g.html*

Al-Hilālī and Khan translation. **University of Northumbria's Islamic Society, About Islam and Muslims**

*http://www.unn.ac.uk/societies/islamic/*

**Humanities Text Initiative, University of Michigan**
*http://www.hti.umich.edu*
**Hong Kong Islamic Youth Organisation**
*http://www.glink.net.hk/~hkiya/c_quran.html*
***The Koran*, trans. M. H. Shakir**
*http://www.hti.umich.edu/relig/koran*
**Le Saint Coran**
*http://www.orst.edu/groups/msa/quran/search_f.html*
**Mosque of the Internet**
*http://www.mosque.com*
**Muslim Students Association of the University of Southern California**
*http://www.usc.edu/dept/MSA/quran/qmtintro.html*
**Qur'ān Comparative Browser**
*http://goon.stg.brown.edu/quran_browser/pqeasy.shtml*
**Qur'ani Tukufu**
*http://www.geocities.com/Athens/Parthenon/2355/*
**Radio al-Islam**
*http://www.islam.org/Radio/*
**Il Sacro Corano**
*http://www.geocities.com/Athens/Forum/8919/framec.htm*
**El Sagrado Corán**
*http://www.orst.edu/groups/msa/quran/index_s.html*
**Türkçe Kuran**
*http://www.bilginet.com/kuran/1kuran.html*

## The Qur'ān: CD-ROM

*The Alim* (USA: ISL Software Corporation, n.d.).

## Books

Ahmed, Akbar S. and Hastings Donnan (eds.). *Islam, Globalization and Postmodernity* (London: Routledge, 1994).

Al-Azmeh, Aziz. *Islam and Modernities* (London and New York: Verso, 1993).

Carey, James W. *Communication as Culture: Essays on Media and Society* (London: Unwin Hyman, 1989).

*Encyclopedia of Islam: New Edition*, I–IX (Leiden: E. J. Brill, 1960– ).

Eickelman, Dale F. and James Piscatori. *Muslim Politics* (Princeton: Princeton University Press, 1996)

al-Fārūqī, Ismā'īl Rājī. *Towards Islamic English* (Herndon: International Institute of Islamic Thought, 1986).

Gibson, William. *Neuromancer* (London: Gollancz, 1984).

Hafner, K. and M. Lyon. *Where Wizards Stay up Late: The Origin of the Internet* (New York: Simon & Schuster, 1996).

Hiro, Dilip. *Islamic Fundamentalism* (London: Paladin Grafton Books, 1988).

Holmes, David (ed.). *Virtual Politics: Identity and Community in Cyberspace* (London, Thousand Oaks, California, New Delhi: Sage Publications, 1997).

Jones, Steven G. (ed.). *Cybersociety: Computer-Mediated Communication and Community* (Thousand Oaks, California, London and New Delhi: Sage Publications, 1995).

Keddie, Nikki. *Roots of Revolution* (New Haven: Yale University Press, 1991).

Kennedy, Angus J. *The Internet: The Rough Guide 1999* (London and New York: Rough Guides Ltd, 1998).

Krol, Ed. *The Whole Internet* (Sebastopol, California: O'Reilly & Associates, Inc., second edn, 1994).

Loader, Brian D. *The Governance of Cyberspace* (Thousand Oaks, California, London and New Delhi: Sage Publications, 1997).

Macdonald, A. M. (ed.). *Chambers Twentieth Century Dictionary* (London: Chambers, 1977).

Marsden, Peter. *The Taliban: War, Religion and the New Order in Afghanistan* (Karachi, Lahore and Islamabad: Oxford University Press; London and New York: Zed Books, 1998).

Metcalf, Barbara Daly. *Making Muslim Space in North America and Europe* (Berkeley and London: University of California Press, 1996).

Mohammadi, Ali (ed.). *International Communication and Globalization: A Critical Introduction* (London, Thousand Oaks, California and New Delhi: Sage Publications, 1997).

Mowlana, Hamid. *Global Communication in Transition: The End of Diversity* (London, Thousand Oaks, California and New Delhi: Sage Publications, 1996).

Netton, Ian Richard. *A Popular Dictionary of Islam* (London: Curzon Press, 1991).

Otto, Rudolf. *The Idea of the Holy: An Inquiry into the Non-rational Factor in the Idea of the Divine and its Relation to the Rational*, trans. John W. Harvey (London and New York: H. Milford; Oxford University Press, 1923).

Rheingold, Howard. *The Virtual Community: Finding Connection in a Computerized World* (London: Secker & Warburg, 1994).

Schimmel, Annemarie. *Deciphering the Signs of God: A Phenomenological Approach to Islam* (Edinburgh: Edinburgh University Press, 1994).

Simpson, John and Tira Shubart, *Lifting the Veil: Life in Revolutionary Iran* (London: Hodder & Stoughton, 1995).

Smart, Ninian. *The World Religions* (Cambridge: Cambridge University Press, 1989).

Strate, Lance, Ronald Jacobson and Stephanie B. Gibson (eds.). *Communication and Cyberspace: Social Interaction in an Electronic Environment* (Cresskill, New Jersey: Hampton Press Inc., 1996).

## Chapters in books

Mitra, Ananda. 'Virtual Commonality: Looking for India on the Internet', in Steven G. Jones, *Virtual Culture: Identity and Communication in Cybersociety* (Thousand Oaks, California: Sage Publications, 1997).

Tehranian, Majid. 'Taming Modernity: Towards a New Paradigm', in Ali Mohammadi (ed.), *International Communication and Globalization: A Critical Introduction* (London, Thousand Oaks, California and New Delhi: Sage Publications, 1997).

## Articles in printed academic journals

Bunt, Gary R. 'Islam in Cyberspace: Islamic Studies Resources on the Internet', *Muslim World Book Review*, 18, 1 (1997).

Kessler, Clive S. 'New Directions in the Study of Islam: Remarks on Some Trends and Prospects', *Jurnal Antropologi Dan Sosiologi*, 18 (1990), 3–22.

## Articles from Internet sources

'Aalim Network. 'Wearing Gold/Najasat of Dogs', 14 June 1998, e-mail list. Sender:
*owner-abdg-a@lists.Stanford.EDU*

Ahmad, Huma. 'Muslims on the Internet: the Good, the Bad . . . the Ugly'.
**Huma Ahmad**
*http://www.jannah.org/me/internet.html*

Ahmadi, Ahmad, Ayatullah Muhammad Hadi M'arifat, Baha al-Din Khorramshahi, Muhammad Husayn Ruhani, Abul Qasim Imami and 'Abbas Zaryab Khoi. 'The Geography of Qur'anic Accounts: Eight Questions from Six Scholars of the Qur'an', trans. from 'Geografiyaye Qisas-e Qur'an', *Bayyinat*, 3.
**Al Islam**
*http://www.al-islam.org/allah/index.html*

Akdeniz, Yaman. 'What is wrong with Internet Rating Systems and Filtering Software', *The Chronicle*, June 1998.
**The Chronicle**
*http://www.thechronicle.demon.co.uk/archive/filter.htm*

Chandler, Daniel. 'Personal Home Pages', 18 August 1998.
**Daniel Chandler**
*http://www.aber.ac.uk/~dgc/webident.html*
Ad-Darsh, Shaykh, 16 August 1996.
**Shaykh Ad-Darsh Column**
*http://ireland.iol.ie/~afifi/Ad-Darsh/16.8.96.htm*
14 March 1997
*http://ireland.iol.ie/~afifi/Ad-Darsh/14.3.97.htm*
Deedat, Aḥmed. 'His Holiness Plays Hide and Seek with Muslims'.
**Ahmed Deedat: Hear His Voice**
*http://home2.swipnet.se/~w–20479/Hide.htm*
Federation of Khoja Shī'a Ithnā 'Asharī Jamaats of Africa. 'HIV and AIDS Make their Presence Felt in the Community', *Samachar*, 31, 1 (September 1998).
**Federation of Khoja Shī'a Ithnā 'Asharī Jamaats of Africa**
*http://www.africafederation.org/fedsamachar/sep98_index.htm*
Halal Foundation. 'A Guide to Halal Food Selection', Illinois: Islamic Food and Nutrition Council of America, n.d.
**University of Houston Muslim Students' Association**
*http://www.uh.edu/campus/msa/articles/halal.html*
Hezb-e Wahdat, 'A Short Biography of the Martyred Leader, Abdul Ali Mazari, R.A.'
**Hazara Press/Hezb-e Wahdat**
*http://www.hazara.com/*
JAKIM. 'Deviationist Teachings in Malaysia'.
**JAKIM**
*http://www.islam.gov.my/*
Jamā'at i Islāmī Pakistan, 'Saying Merry Christmas to Christians', 16 December 1998
**Jamā'at i Islāmī**
*http://www.jamaat.org/*
*(deleted article)*
_____. 'JI moot adopts charter for women', 24 October 1998
*http://www.jamaat.org/news/newsarchive98/pr102498.html*
_____. 'What is wrong with Motorway?', 16 December 1998
*http://www.jamaat.org/ (deleted article)*
_____. 'Jamaat poised for ouster of Nawaz-government ', 14 November 1998
*http://www.jamaat.org/news/newsarchive98/pr111498.html*
Ibrahim, Anwar. 'The Asian Renaissance' (n.d.).
**Anwar Ibrahim and Gerakan Reformasi Malaysia**
*http://reformasi.cjb.net*

Khan, Liaquat Ali. 'Islam and the Web'.
**CyberMomin**
*http://www.geocities.com/Athens/Oracle/5118/IslamWeb.htm*
Khomeini, Hojjatoleslam Seyyed Hassan. Speech during visit to Islamic Republic News Agency (IRNA), Tehran, 3 June 1998.
**IRNA**
*http://www.irna.com/ertehal/visit.html*
Lakha, Amir G. N., 'Why the need for a Jiba Web Site'.
**JIBA Europe**
*http://www.jiba.org/*
Masjid Tucson United Submitters International. 'Challenging the Qur'an. What went wrong!'
**Masjid Tucson United Submitters International**
*http://www.submission.org/challenge.html*
McLuhan, Marshall. Transcript of lecture at Florida State University, 1970.
**VideoMcLuhan**
*http://www.videomcluhan.com/lectures.htm*
MIRA. 'Dispatches from Behind the Veil'.
**MIRA**
*http://www.miraserve.com/arabia/a5h2.htm*
Al-Muhajiroun. 'The Policy of Al-Muhajiroun in The West'.
**Al-Muhajiroun**
*www.almuhajiroun.com*
Murad, Abdal Hakim. 'British and Muslim?'
**Belfast Islamic Centre**
*http://ireland.iol.ie/~afifi/Articles/british.htm*
Muzaffar, Chandra. 'ADIL Answers Five Supreme Ironies', 26 January 1999.
**ADIL - Gerakan Reformasi**
*http://members.easyspace.com/reformasi/answer2.htm*
Negroponte, Nicholas. 'Beyond Digital', *Wired*, 6.12 (December 1998).
**Wired**
*http://nicholas.www.media.mit.edu/people/nicholas/Wired/WIRED6–12.html*
*As Sahwa*, 'Fatwa or Divine Decree concerning Salman Rushdie', *As Sahwa* 2:11 (October 1998).
**Al Muhajiroun**
*http://www.almuhajiroun.com*
_____. 'British Government's New Laws to Stop Islamic Activity!' *As Sahwa* 2:13 (December 1998).
*http://www.almuhajiroun.com*
_____. 'Muslims will Hound Blair Wherever he Goes!' *As Sahwa* 2:14 (January 1999).
*http://www.almuhajiroun.com*

Whine, Michael. 'Islamist Organisations on the Internet' (April 1998). **The International Policy Institute for Counter-Terrorism** *http://www.ict.org.il/articles/articledet.cfm?articleid=31*

## Articles in magazines

Rathmell, Andrew. 'Netwar in the Gulf', *Jane's Intelligence Review* (January 1997), 29–32.

Zobel, Gibby. 'A New Kind of Revolution', *The Big Issue*, 11–17 January 1999.

## News sources

BBC News. 'Iranian Conservative Slams Internet', 23 January 1999 *http://news2.thdo.bbc.co.uk/hi/english/world/middle%5Feast/newsid%5F261000/261300.stm*

_____. 'Ayatollah Khomeini on the Web', 2 June 1998 *http://news2.thdo.bbc.co.uk/hi/english/world/middle%5Feast/newsid%5F104000/104312.stm*

_____. 'Surfing in the Desert', 6 May 1998 *http://news2.thdo.bbc.co.uk/hi/english/sci/tech/newsid%5F88000/88821.stm*

_____. 'Indian Army Website Ambushed', 16 October 1998 *http://news2.thdo.bbc.co.uk/hi/english/world/south%5Fasia/newsid%5F194000/194844.stm*

_____. 'US CyberTerrorism Plea', 22 January 1999 *http://news2.thdo.bbc.co.uk/hi/english/world/americas/newsid%5F260000/260855.stm*

_____. Nuttall, Chris, 'Virtual Country "nuked" on Net', 26 January 1999 *http://news2.thdo.bbc.co.uk/hi/english/sci/tech/newsid%5F263000/263169.stm*

*The Christian Science Monitor*. Scott Peterson, 'Iran's Newest Revolution: Holy Texts Go On Computer', 13 October 1998 *http://www.csmonitor.com/*

Inter Press Service. 'Sudan-Internet: Muslim Sect Sees "Moral Pollution" on Internet', 16 March 1998 (link deleted)

IRNA Iranian News Agency. 'late-imam-works-internet', 2 June 1998 *http://www.irna.com/newshtm/eng/11163523.htm* (link deleted)

Reuters Press Agency. 'Malaysian Technological Sufis Await Islam Messiah', July 13, 1994

_____. 'Saudi Arabia Launches Internet', 25 January 1999

Stone, Paul. 'Internet Presents Web of Security Issues', American Forces Press Service.
**American Forces Information Service**
*http://www.defenselink.mil/news*
September 1998.

## Thesis

Bunt, G. R. 'Decision-making and *Idjtihād* in Islamic Environments: a comparative study of Pakistan, Malaysia, Singapore, and the United Kingdom' (Lampeter: University of Wales, Ph.D., 1997).

## CD-ROM

*Islamic Gateway,* version 2.6 (London, 1998).
*Microsoft Flight Simulator 98,* CD-ROM (Microsoft Corporation, 1997).

## Interviews

Ahmad, Anis. Interview with writer, 30 April 1995. Da'wa Academy, International Islamic University, Islamabad.
Ahmed, Monzur. E-mail response to writer's questions, 5 December 1998.
Al-'Akiti, M. 'Afifi. Belfast Islamic Centre, e-mail response to writer's questions, 5 June 1998.
Khayat, Ossama M. Tawhid Islamic Movement in Lebanon, 15 June 1998, e-mail response to writer's questions.
Rawji, Mustafa. Co-administrator, 'Aalim Network, e-mail response to writer's questions, 10 August 1998.

## Internet sites: Uniform Resource Locators (URLs)

Generic site titles are provided alphabetically here. Proper names are listed under first names (i.e. Anwar Ibrahim is under 'A' rather than 'I'). Original spellings for all site titles are provided. Check the Virtually Islamic website for updated hyperlinks.

**A Card for Anwar Ibrahim**
*http://cardforanwar.hypermart.net/*
**ABIM Online**
*http://www.jaring.my/abim/english/index.html*

**Ahlul Bayt Digital Islamic Library Project (DILP)/Al-Islam**
*http://www.al-islam.org/allah/index.html*
**Aḥmed Deedat: Hear His Voice**
*http://home2.swipnet.se/~w–20479/Audio.htm*
**Altavista**
*http://altavista.digital.com*
**Answering Christianity**
*http://www.angelfire.com/ak/BaltoMuslims/answers.html*
**Answering Islam**
*http://answering-islam.org/*
*http://answering-islam.org.uk*
**Answer to Answering Islam**
*http://www.submission.org/answering-islam-org.htm*
**Anwar Ibrahim**
*http://anwaribrahim1.com/*
**Anwar Ibrahim and Gerakan Reformasi Malaysia**
*http://reformasi.cjb.net*
**ArabNet**
*http://www.arab.net/links/yn/welcome.html*
**Arab Information Project at Georgetown University**
*http://www.georgetown.edu/research/arabtech/*
**Ask Jeeves**
*http://www.askjeeves.com/*
**Ask the Imam**
*http://islam.org/islamicity/dialogue/a1.htm*
**Attasia Tarīkah**
*http://www.attasia.org*
**Al-Azhar**
*http://www.alazhar.org*
**Baltimore Muslims**
*http://www.angelfire.com/ak/BaltoMuslims/advicefornew.html*
**Belfast Islamic Centre**
*http://ireland.iol.ie/~afifi/*
**Bosanski Webring**
*http://www.webring.org/cgi-bin/webring?ring=bosnjaci;index*
**Bosnet**
*http://www.bosnet.org/*
**Bosnia-Net**
*http://www.fama.com*
**Cat Stevens**
*http://catstevens.com/*
**CDLR**
*http://www.ummah.org.uk/cdlr/*

**Chishti Habibi Soofie Islamic Order**
*http://www.soofie.org.za/*
**Chisti Qadhiri**
*http://www.geocities.com/Athens/Olympus/5352/geobook.html*
**CIA World Factbook**
*http://www.odci.gov/cia/publications/factbook/*
**Committee against Corruption in Saudi Arabia (CACSA)**
*http://www.saudhouse.com/frontmen.htm*
**Complete Guide to Palestine's Websites**
*http://www.birzeit.edu/links*
**Constitutionalists Movement of Iran**
*http://www.irancmi.org/index3.htm*
**CyberSalat**
*http://www.ummah.net/software/cyber/*
**Dar ul-Iman**
*http://www.chishti.com/*
**Department of Islamic Development of Malaysia, Prime Minister's Department (JAKIM)**
*http://www.islam.gov.my/profail/BI/profile.html*
**Dhikr in Congregation: Khatm-ul-Khwajagan**
*http://www.naqshbandi.org/frmpract.htm*
**DiWani**
'Subahallah Alhamdullliah', *Jalan Yang Satu*
*http://islamicbookstore.com/islamic_audios/islamic_songs.shtml*
**Doctrine of Ahl Al-Sunna versus the 'Salafi' Movement**
*http://www.naqshbandi.org/ottomans/wahhabis.htm*
**Excite**
*http://www.excite.com*
**Front Islamique du Salut**
*http://www.fisalgeria.org*
**Godlas, Alan. 'Islamic Art, Music and Architecture'**
*http://www.arches.uga.edu/~godlas/IslArt.html*
**Hamas**
*http://www.hamas.org*
**Hezbollah**
*http://www.hezbollah.org/*
**Hizb ut-Tahrir**
*http://www.hizb-ut-tahrir.com/*
**Hizbollah Central Press Office**
*http://www.hizbollah.org/hizb/definiti.html*
**Idara Dawat-O-Irshad USA Inc.**
*http://irshad.org/idara/home.htm*
**Image of Sunshine**
*http://www.irna.com/ertehal/images/family-e.htm*

**IKIM, Institut Kefahaman Islam Malaysia**
*http://www.ikim.gov.my/s301–7.htm*
**IslamicBookstore**
*http://islamicbookstore.com/*
**IslamiCity**
*http://islamicity.org/*
**Islam-Iran**
*http://www.islam-iran.org/foundations/link17.htm*
**Islamic Affairs Department, Royal Embassy of Saudi Arabia**
*http://www.iad.org/*
**Islamic Assembly of North America (IANA), Fatwa and Research Centre**
*http://www.iananet.org/fatwa/fatwa.html*
**Islamic Association of Palestine**
*http://www.iap.org*
**Islamic Audio Studio (IAS), Islamic Centre of Blacksburg, Virginia**
*http://www.bev.net/community/sedki/icb_ra.html*
**Islamic Centre of England (London)**
*http://www.ic-el.org/*
**Islamic Finder**
*http://www.islamicfinder.org/finder/*
**IslamFirst**
*http://www.angelfire.com/al/islamfirst/*
**Islamic Gateway**
*http://www.ummah.net/aboutig.html*
**Islamic Network**
*http://www.isnet.org*
**Islamic Republic of Pakistan**
*http://www.pak.gov.pk/*
**Islamic Studies Pathways**
*http://www.lamp.ac.uk/cis/pathways*
**JAKIM (Ruangan Soal Jawab Agama bersama Jabatan Kemajuan Islam Malaysia)**
*http://www.islam.gov.my/*
**Jamiat-e-Islami Afghanistan**
*http://www.jamiat.com/goals/goal.html*
**Jamā'at i Islāmī Pakistan**
*http://www.jamaat.org*
**JIBA Europe**
*http://www.jiba.org*
**JKLF**
*http://www.geocities.com/CapitolHill/Lobby/8125/fpage.html*

**Al Kassam Shuhada Memorial**
*http://www.demon.co.uk/alquds/*
**Al-Khoei Foundation**
*http://www.al-khoei.org/updates.htm*
**Khoja Shī'a Ithnā 'Asharī World Federation**
*http://www.world-federation.org*
**King Faisal Foundation**
*http://www.kff.com/*
**Laman Reformasi**
*http://members.tripod.com/~mahazalim/*
**Lycos City Guide: Makkah**
*http://cityguide.lycos.com/middle_east/arabian_peninsula/SAUMakkah.html*
**Majlis Ugama Islam Singapura**
*http://www.muis.gov.sg*
***Ma'rifat***
*http://www.qabas.net/marifat/*
**Al-Moukhtar**
*http://www.al-mokhtar.com.lb/friday.htm*
**Al-Muhājiroun**
*www.almuhajiroun.com*
**Mulid of Egypt**
*http://www.microstate.com/mm/mulid/*
(link deleted)
**Muslim Converts' Association of Singapore (Darul Arqam Singapore)**
*http://www.darul-arqam.org.sg/*
**Muslim Hackers' Homepage**
*http://www.ummah.net/mhc*
**Muslims Online**
*http://www.muslimsonline.com/*
**Muslim Students Association, University of Missouri-Rolla**
*http://www.umr.edu/~msaumr/topics/.*
**Muttahida Quami Movement (MQM)**
*http://www.mqm.org*
**Naqshbandi Sufi Way**
*http://www.naqshbandi.org/frmabout.htm*
**Official Ali Shariati Site**
*http://www.shariati.com*
**Online Islamic Propagation Team**
*http://members.aol.com/Palestine5/*
**Pakistan People's Party**
*http://www.ppp.org.pk*

**Pakistan Tehreek-e-Insaf**
*http://www.insaf.com/*
**Palestine Information Centre**
*http://www.palestine-info.org*
**Parti Islam Semalaysia (PAS)**
*http://www.jaring.my/pas*
**PAS Johore**
*http://www.geocities.com/CapitolHill/Senate/5059/a_rasmi.htm*
**Philosophy in Cyberspace, Monash University (personal pages), Australia**
*http://www-personal.monash.edu.au/~dey/phil/section1.htm*
**Prime Minister's Office of Malaysia**
*http://www.smpke.jpm.my/*
**Qabas**
*http://www.qabas.net*
**Queer Jihad**
*http://www.geocities.com/WestHollywood/Heights/8977/index*
**Queer Muslims**
*http://www.angelfire.com/ca2/queermuslims/*
**Quotations from Famous Historians of Science**
*http://www.erols.com/zenithco/Introl1.html#refer1*
**Quraan and Islamic Sciences City**
*http://members.tripod.com/Flowersun/home.html*
**Radio Islam**
*http://abbc.com/islam/english/english.htm*
**Ramadhan**
*http://www.ramadhan.org*
**RealNetworks**
*http://www.real.com/*
**Revolutionary Association of the Women of Afghanistan (RAWA)**
*http://www.rawa.org/*
**Royal Malaysian Naqshbandi Group**
'Praising the Prophet: The Mawlid'
*http://www.naqshbandi.org/frmpract.htm*
**Shīʻa Ismaili Web**
*http://www.hal-pc.org/~amana/ismaili.html*
**Shīʻa Muslim Salams, Marsiyas and Nohas**
*http://www.geocities.com/Athens/Agora/9220/*
**Sufi Fighting Arts Movie Production (Islamic)**
*http://www.ummah.net/fighting/movie.htm*
**Sufism in Indonesia**
*http://www.geocities.com/Athens/5738/frame.htm*
**Ṣūfī Order of the West**
*http://www.sufiorder.org/indexie.html*

**Sun's House**
*http://www.irna.com/occasion/ertehal/index-e.htm*
**SuraLikeIt UK**
*http://dspace.dial.pipex.com/suralikeit*
**Tajweed**
*http://www.duke.edu/~maa3/Tajweed/Taj.html*
**Taleban Islamic Movement of Afghanistan**
*http://www.taleban.com*
**Taliban Online**
*http://www.ummah.net/dharb/*
**Tanzeem-e-Islami Pakistan**
*http://www.tanzeem.org.pk*
**The Reformation Movement Starts Here!**
*http://www.cyberway.com.sg/~nassir/*
**Tijaniyya Tariqat**
*http://www.geocities.com/Athens/9189/shhassan.html*
**UMNO Youth Movement**
*http://www.umnoyouth.org.my*
**United Muslims of America**
*http://fortyhadith.khomeini.com/*
**'Unofficial' Al-Azhar Page**
*http://www.ims.uwindsor.ca/~azhar/*
**US Muslim Students Association of the University of Southern California**
*http://www.usc.edu/dept/MSA/quran/qmtintro.html*
**WAMY**
*http://www.wamy.org/*
**Webcrawler**
*http://www.webcrawler.com/*
**Webpress Alternative**
*http://www.webpres.com.my/malaysia*
**Yahoo!**
*http://www.yahoo.com*
**Yusuf Qaradawi**
*http://www.qaradawi.net*
**Zipple**
*http://www.zipple.com/*

## Other material from websites

Ciriello, A. Raffaele. *Photographs of Afghan Women*
**Afghanistan Online**
*http://www.afghan-web.com/ciriello/woman*

Ibn Rushd, Abū 'l-Walīd Muḥammad b. Aḥmad. *Bidayat al-Mujtahid wa Kifayat al-Muqtasid.*

**Belfast Islamic Centre**

*http://ireland.iol.ie/~afifi/Ilm/Fiqh/BidayatMujtahid/Contents.htm*

Kabbani, Shaykh Muḥammad Hisham. 'History and Guidebook of the Saints of the Golden Chain'.

**The Naqshbandi Sufi Way**

*http://www.naqshbandi.net/haqqani/sufi/NaqshSufiWay/Sh_Nazim.html*

al-Nawawī, Imam. *'Al-Maqasid'*, trans. Noah Ha Mim Keller.

***Al Maqasid***

*http://www.nbic.org/isru/Resources/Maqasid/*

Rayes, Mohamed. E-mail contribution to 'soc.religion.islam' discussion group, 23 June 1998.

Al-Seestani, Ayatullāh al-'Uzma al-Sayyid 'Ali al-Husayni. 'Contemporary Legal Rulings in Shī'a Law in accordance with the Rulings (Fatāwā) of Ayatullāh al-'Uzma al-Sayyid 'Ali al-Husayni al-Seestani'.

**Al-Islam**

*http://www.al-islam.org/laws/contemporary/index.html*

al-Shaafi'i, Al-Imaam Muhammad ibn Idris. *Ar-Risaalah Fee Usool al-Fiqh*, trans. M. Khadduri (Cambridge: Islamic Texts Society)

**Islamic Texts Society**

*http://www.islaam.com/articles/sunnah_shafi1.htm*

# *Glossary*

| | |
|---|---|
| *adhān* | call to prayer |
| *aḥādīth* | the body of traditional sayings (and/or reports of the actions) of Muḥammad (cf. *ḥadīth*). |
| *Ahl Qur'ān wa 'l Sunna* | People of the Qur'ān and Sunna (tradition) |
| *Ahl al-Sunna* | People of Sunna or 'tradition'; Sunnī Muslims |
| *āyāt* | (singular: *āya*) verses of the Qur'ān, 'sign' (cf. *Sūra*) |
| *Āyatullāh* | literally the 'sign of God'; within Shī'a Islam (q.v.) this can denote the rank of a highly qualified interpreter of Islamic jurisprudence |
| *Aḥmadiyah* | a sect within Islam, sometimes referred to as the Qādianīs, which contains a number of branches, and is ostracized by many within 'mainstream' Islam for the messianic claims of its founded Ghulām Aḥmad (d. 1908). |
| *'ālim* | a scholar (cf. *'ulamā'*) |
| *arkān al-Islam* | pillars or foundations of Islam (marked * in this Glossary) |
| *Al-Azhar* | mosque and university located in Cairo, and widely regarded as an academic centre of excellence within Sunnī Islam |
| *Basmala* | this is the title of the phrase frequently utilized in prayer and in the Qur'ān: in full, the phrase is *Bismi'llāh al-Raḥmān al-Raḥīm*, which can be translated as 'In the Name of God, the Compassionate, the Merciful'. |
| *bay'ā* | a pledge of allegiance |
| *Chistiyya* | a branch of Ṣūfī Islam (q.v.) |

| | |
|---|---|
| *da'wa* | the propagation of Islam |
| *dhikr* | the repetition or remembrance of Qur'ānic phrases, or the names of God, especially in Ṣūfī Islam (q.v.) |
| *du'a* | (supererogatory) prayer |
| *fatwā* | the opinions of specific *imāms* (q.v.) and *Āyatullāhs* (q.v.). (pl. *fatāwā*) |
| *fiqh* | Islamic jurisprudence |
| *ḥadīth* | a traditional saying (and/or report of the actions) of Muḥammad (cf. *aḥādīth*) |
| *ḥāfiz* | a title denoting one who had learnt the Qur'ān by heart. |
| *ḥajj* | the major pilgrimage to Mecca* |
| *ḥalāl* | a term applied to denote that which is appropriate or permitted within the bounds of Islam |
| *Ḥizb Allāh* | Party of God (also transliterated *Hezbollah/Hizbollah*) |
| *Ḥizb ut-Ṭahrīr* | Party of Purity |
| *Ibrāhīm* | Abraham |
| *'Īd al-Fiṭr* | the concluding feast of *Ramaḍān* (q.v.) |
| *ijtihād* | independent judgement based on Islamic sources; interpretation of primary sources in light of contemporary conditions |
| *'ilm al-tajwīd* | the science of recitation (of the Qur'ān) |
| *imām* | the term *imām* usually refers to one who leads the prayers, not necessarily 'qualified' in the sense of trained clergy. In Shī'ā Islam (q.v.), *Imām* has associations with religious leadership *and* continuity of spiritual authority |
| *Islām* | literally 'submission' to God. |
| *Ismā'īlī* | a form of Shī'ā Islam (q.v.), which itself fragmented to form disparate branches (including the Fāṭimids, the Nizīris, the Assassins, Bohorās) |
| *Ithnā 'Asharīs* | literally the 'Twelvers', a form of Shī'ā Islam (q.v.) |
| *Jamā'at-i Islāmī* | synonymous with a Pakistani political party; the term is applied elsewhere, and implies a congregation, collective or party (of Islam) |

| | |
|---|---|
| *jihād* | 'striving' to attain an Islamic objective; the term has spiritual and/or militaristic connotations |
| *jihād bil-sayf* | *jihād* (q.v.) (with the sword) |
| *jinn* | ethereal beings, mentioned several times in the Qur'ān |
| *jum'a* | Friday prayers |
| *Ka'ba* | the 'holy house' (in Mecca). |
| *Khalīfa* | (pl. *khulafa'*) caliph, vice-regent, successor to Muḥammad (q.v.) |
| *kufr* | non-belief (in Islam) |
| *mu'adhdhin* | muezzin, one who makes the *adhān* (q.v.) |
| *madhhab* | a school of Islamic interpretation |
| *al-Mahdī* | the rightly guided one |
| *masjid* | mosque, place of prayer |
| *Masjid Al-Quds* | Mosque of Jerusalem |
| *mawlid* | birthday of Muḥammad *and/or* anniversary of saints |
| *minbar* | the mosque equivalent of a pulpit |
| *al-Muhājirūn* | the migrants from Mecca at the time of Muḥammad, who provided him with support during the early period of Islam. (ii) The title is applied by an activist platform, Al-Muhājiroun, located in the United Kingdom |
| Muḥammad | Muḥammad ibn 'Abd Allāh, the Prophet of Islam (*c.* 570–632 CE) (cf. Qur'ān) |
| *mujtahid* | an interpreter of Muslim law |
| *murīd* | a follower, usually in the context of Ṣūfī Islam (q.v.) |
| *mushāf* | the definitive recension of the Qur'ān |
| *mutajwīd* | reciters of the Qur'ān |
| *Naqshbandī* | a branch of Ṣūfī Islam (q.v.) |
| *nashīd*s | this genre extends from sung versions of *aḥādīth* to Ṣūfī Naqshbandī (q.v.) 'sung' prayers, and popular Islamic music |
| *qasīda* | a pledge of allegiance (cf. *bay'ā*) |
| *Qur'ān* | Revelation received by the Prophet Muḥammad, via the Angel Gabriel |
| *Ramaḍān* | Month of fasting, and the month in which the Qur'ān was revealed (cf. *ṣawm*) |
| *raka'āt* | prayer sequences, positions, units of prayer |

| | |
|---|---|
| *ribā* | capital interest, usury |
| *ṣawm* | fasting in Ramaḍān (q.v.)* |
| *ṣalāt* | prayer* |
| *shahāda* | the principle of proclaiming a belief in One God whose Final Prophet is Muḥammad* |
| *shahīd* | martyr |
| *shaykh* | religious leader, leader of a *ṭarīqa* (q.v.) |
| *sharīʻa* | law based on Islamic sources |
| *Shīʻa* | literally 'the party' or followers of the (line of) ʻAlī ibn Abī Ṭālib |
| *Ṣūfī* | Muslim mystic; the term has broad connotations and definitions, within disparate branches of Islam (cf. *taṣawwuf*). |
| *Sunnī* | 'orthodox' Islam, based on the *sunna* (q.v.) |
| *sunna* | the actions of Muḥammad (cf. *aḥādīth*) |
| *Sūra, Sūrat* | a chapter within the Qur'ān (pl. *Suwar*) (cf. *āyāt*) |
| *tafsīr* | commentary (on the Qur'ān) |
| *ṭarīqa* | literally a 'path', generally a term associated with *Ṣūfī* Orders |
| *taṣawwuf* | esoteric Islam, Ṣūfism (cf. *Ṣūfī*) |
| *tawḥīd* | Unity (of God) |
| *'ulamā'* | scholars (cf. *'ālim*) |
| *umma* | Muslim community |
| *zakāt* | annual alms taxation* |
| *Zaydī* | a branch of Shīʻa Islam |

# Index